KU-204-557

Contents

CONTENTS

Introducing the Costa Blanca

Many visitors to the Costa Blanca come looking for an all-inclusive beach holiday in the sun. And while nowhere in Europe is more consciously devoted to catering to their tastes the area offers plenty more besides.

If you're looking for an easy, cheap beach holiday nowhere in Europe offers more choice than the Costa Blanca. Benidorm is the biggest resort in the Mediterranean and the tourist conurbation that has grown up around the town has been living off the package beach holiday for almost 50 years. It now provides sea-and-sun packages with the efficiency, cut-price and quality of service of a large supermarket chain. The beaches are superb, if rarely deserted, and theme parks, day excursions, variety shows, thumping dance clubs, bingo halls, bars and pubs ensure that there's familiar entertainment for everyone from children to adults.

But there's another Costa Blanca too—inland and away from the mega-resorts, which is quieter, more intimate and far more Spanish. A short drive from the crowded coast are sleepy Moorish towns like Jativa and Mula, whose tile and terracotta roofs cluster and crowd around craggy castles set in romantic hills. The modern, industrial hinterlands of towns like Elche and Orihuela hide glorious Renaissance centres filled with grand baroque churches and imperial civic buildings on stately plazas. Many still host lively and very Spanish festivals—like Alcoy's splendid Moros y Cristianos crusader pageant—where foreign tourists remain few and far between and it's still possible to lose yourself in a Spanish crowd. There are stretches of wilderness too: the rugged Sierra de Espuña hills, and the lonely beaches and coves of the Calblanque coast.

The Costa Blanca falls into three main regions. The northern area around Benidorm, the central area around the castle town of Alicante and the southern area around the pretty Renaissance city of Murcia. You could drive from north to south in less than half a day.

Facts + Figures

- **Residents: 2.5 million people.**
- **Only 50 per cent were born of local parents.**
- **More than 70 per cent of homeowners are foreign.**

SUNSHINE

The Costa Blanca is one of the sunniest parts of southern Europe. The northern region around Benidorm enjoys 3,147 hours of sunshine per year, the southern around Murcia, 3,098. As most visitors know, it is essential to take precautions to avoid sunburn.

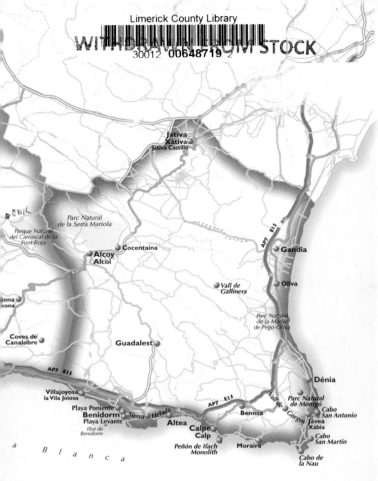

TWINPACK
Costa Blanca

ALEX ROBINSON

If you have any comments
or suggestions for this guide
you can contact the editor at
Twinpacks@theAA.com

AA Publishing
Find out more about AA Publishing and the wide
range of services the AA provides by visiting our
website at theAA.com/bookshop

How to Use This Book

KEY TO SYMBOLS

✚	Map reference	▷	Further information
✉	Address	ℹ	Tourist information
☎	Telephone number	✋	Admission charges: Expensive (over €10), Moderate (€3–€10), and Inexpensive (under €3)
⏰	Opening/closing times		
🍴	Restaurant or café	★ Major Sight	★ Minor Sight
🚆	Nearest rail station		
🚌	Nearest bus route	👣 Walks	🚗 Drives
♿	Facilities for visitors with disabilities	🛍 Shops	
❓	Other practical information	🎭 Entertainment and Activities	
		🍴 Restaurants	

This guide is divided into four sections

• **Essential Costa Blanca:** An introduction to the region and tips on making the most of your stay.
• **Costa Blanca by Area:** We've broken the region into three areas, and recommended the best sights, shops, activities, restaurants, entertainment and nightlife venues in each one. Suggested walks and drives help you to explore.
• **Where to Stay:** The best hotels, whether you're looking for luxury, budget or something in between.
• **Need to Know:** The info you need to make your trip run smoothly, including getting about by public transport, weather tips, emergency phone numbers and useful websites.

Navigation In the Costa Blanca by Area chapter, we've given each area its own colour, which is also used on the locator maps throughout the book and the map on the inside front cover.

Maps The fold-out map accompanying this book is a comprehensive map of the Costa Blanca. The grid on this fold-out map is the same as the grid on the locator maps within the book. The grid references to these maps are shown with capital letters, for example A1. The grid references to the Alicante and Murcia town plans are shown with lower-case letters, for example a1.

VALENCIAN LANGUAGE

The official language of the Costa Blanca is Spanish. Valencian in widely spoken in and around Benidorm and Alicante and boasts more than 2 million speakers. Valencian is a romance language resembling both Catalan and Castillian Spanish but distinct from both. Many of the tourist offices in the region offer free English-Valencian dictionaries.

DESERTIFICATION

Large stretches of the Costa Blanca are becoming desertified—through global warming and poorly planned development for golf courses and irrigated agriculture. A series of scandals involving the granting of water rights to developers in exchange for bribes has seen government officials in Murcia imprisoned. Rainfall is predicted to fall by 20 per cent from 2008 to 2020, and 40 per cent by 2070, according to the UN.

A Short Stay on the Costa Blanca

DAY 1: BENIDORM AND THE NORTH

Morning Stay on **Playa Levante beach** (▷ 56). Wake early at around 7 and stroll down to the sea for a sunbathe and refreshing swim before the sun gets too intense and the sand gets crowded. Return after and hour or so for breakfast in the hotel. Spend the rest of the morning exploring the old fishing village.

Lunch Sit for a leisurely early lunch at one of the numerous little bar cafes that line the Avenida de Alcoy esplanade next to the beach and while away an hour or so people-watching.

Afternoon Take a coach tour through the Sierra de Aitana behind Benidorm to **Guadalest** (▷ 64–65)—a crumbling medieval fortified village perched on a series of dramatic crags and watching over the shimmering coast. Spend the rest of the afternoon wandering the ruins, browsing the street of boutique shops and visiting the town's **Museo de Microminiatura**, devoted to all things miniature (▷ 65).

Late Afternoon Return to Benidorm in time to watch the sunset from Plaza San Jaume on the promontory between the town's two beaches. And then leisurely walk back to Playa Levante beach along the esplanade. Book a rental car for the following day.

Dinner Eat Valencian seafood or Spanish paella at **La Palmera** (▷ 82) or **Tiffany's** (▷ 82) in Benidorm, accompanied by a Ribera del Duero or a Rioja.

Evening Sample Benidorm's brash but buzzing nightlife at a beach bar, pub, show or one of the dance clubs that lie behind the town.

DAY 2: JATIVA

Morning After an early morning dip in the Mediterranean take a light breakfast and head for the hills and an exploration of the Costa Blanca's wilder, historical hinterland.

Mid-morning Stop for coffee and a goat's cheese with pineapple curry sauce tapas at the **Il Cavacici café** (▷ 81) in **Cocentaina** (▷ 70). Walk around the tiny Renaissance town centre before continuing on to **Jativa** (▷ 66–67), the city of Borgias and site of one of an impressive castle.

Lunch Spend the late morning and early afternoon exploring Játiva's medieval and Moorish old centre. Be sure to visit the various churches and the 15th-century baroque Palácio del Marqués de Motortal and the Casa de Diego. Take a light lunch at one of the plaza cafes and then drive up the road to the castle, stopping off at the beautiful **San Feliu church** (▷ 67) on castle hill.

Afternoon Devote the afternoon to a leisurely tour of the town's magnificent **castle** (▷ 68–69). Begin with the Carthaginian Castillo Menor, to the east, through the castle's Gothic gateway. The Himilce tower is named after Hannibal's wife, who is said to have borne a son here in AD218. Spend the late afternoon in the Moorish and Renaissance western portion of the castle. Wander through the beautiful gardens and visit the Capilla de San Jordi and the Capilla de Santa Maria chapels which preserve the tombs of rulers of two medieval Spanish states. As the sunlight turns a rich golden yellow, take in the glorious views from the battlements out across the plain.

Evening Enjoy some of the best regional cooking on the Costa Blanca at **La Agelma restaurant** (▷ 81) in the shadow of the castle before returning to Benidorm for a nightcap or a final night on the tiles.

Top 25

ESSENTIAL COSTA BLANCA TOP 25

► ► ►

Alcoy ▷ 52 A prosperous inland town with one of Spain's most colourful traditional festivals.

Alicante town ▷ 24–25 Costa Blanca's transport hub and a very Spanish town with great museums.

Alicante: Castillo ▷ 28–29 A fortified hilltop castle with a fascinating history and coastal views.

Sierra de Espuña ▷ 94–95 These hills, the site of one of the world's first re-forestation projects and are a haven for rare wildlife.

Orihuela: Catedral ▷ 36–37 A gorgeous baroque church hidden behind a modest exterior.

Orihuela town ▷ 34–35 This modern town has a fine, beautifully preserved Renaissance centre.

Novelda's Casa-Museo Modernista ▷ 37 This is reminiscent of Gaudí.

Murcia: Catedral ▷ 92–93 One of Spain's largest and most impressive churches.

Murcia ▷ 90–91 The capital of southern Costa Blanca, Murcia is a handsome Renaissance town.

Mula ▷ 89 one of the least spoiled medieval villages; a good access point for the Sierra de Espuña.

Moratalla ▷ 88 A sleepy mountain village in a corner of Murcia with a lively traditional festival.

Jativa's Castillo ▷ 68–69 The Costa Blanca's most impressive castle built along a long hill.

8

These pages are a quick guide to the Top 25, which are described in more detail later. Here they are listed alphabetically, and the tinted background shows which area they are in.

Alicante: Museo Arqueológico ▷ **26–27**
Trace the history of the region from the Stone Age.

Altea ▷ **53** A popular beach resort north of Benidorm with a pretty historical centre.

Benidorm's Beaches ▷ **56** Twin stretches of broad fine sand backed by Europe's busiest resort.

Benidorm town ▷ **54–55** A beach resort city of towering hotels and beer-fuelled nightlife.

Calblanque ▷ **86–87** The quietest and least spoiled stretch of coast.

Calpe ▷ **58–59** This mini-Benidorm is watched over by an impressive monolith.

Dénia ▷ **60–61** Laid-back family resort has pretty beaches and a distinguished history.

Elche ▷ **30** A modern town hiding a glorious Renaissance centre.

Elche: Palmeral ▷ **31** Europe's largest palm forest garden and a UNESCO World Heritage Site.

Gandia ▷ **62–63** A sprawling, old-fashioned resort with a glorious palace museum.

ALICANTE AND AROUND
20–48

BENIDORM AND THE NORTH
49–82

Jativa
Xàtiva
Jativa Castillo

Parc Natural de la Serra Mariola

Parque Natural del Carrascal de la Font Roja

Alcoy
Alcoi

Gandia

Novelda
Casa Museo Modernista

Parc Natural de la Marjal de Pego-Oliva

Elche
Eix
Palmeral

Guadalest

..que
...atural
.l Hondo

Alicante
Alacant

Dénia

astillo de Santa Bárbara,
Museo Arqueológico

Benidorm
Benidorm: Beaches

Altea

Parc Natural de Montgó

Calpe
Calp

Illa de
Tabarca

Costa   Blanca

Illot de
Benidorm

Peñón de Ifach
Monolith

Jativa ▷ **66–67** The best preserved medieval town in the region and the original home of the Borgias.

Illa de Tabarca ▷ **32–33** The sea around these rocky islands offers good snorkelling.

Guadalest ▷ **64–65** A ruined fortified village perched on craggy peaks just inland from Benidorm.

◀ ◀ ◀

9

Finding Peace and Quiet

The Costa Blanca may be the busiest resort area in Mediterranean Europe but even in high season it is surprisingly easy to find a quiet spot in the hills or even along the crowded coast.

Medieval Villages

The rocky hills of the Sierra rise abruptly behind the Costa Blanca beaches. And whilst villages like Guadalest are well-visited there are still numerous sleepy little medieval towns that are quiet enough to hear a footstep. Pocket-sized, medieval Játiva and Cocentaina in the Benidorm region are delightfully tranquil and small-scale, steeped in history and little visited outside peak season. The least-spoiled villages of all are in Murcia. Mula and Moratalla are traditional Spanish towns set in dramatic countryside whose nightlife comprises bodegas and tapas bars rather than booming clubs.

Renaissance Towns

The flat coastal hinterland behind Alicante is dotted with pretty Renaissance towns. Most are peaceful and tourist-free. Magnificent churches, monasteries and palaces built from rich yellow stone fill the streets and tinkling fountain-filled plazas in Orihuela. In the late afternoon the sun burnishes them a rich gold that sets them dramatically against the looming dark green of the mountains that rise steeply behind the city. Nearby Elche also has an attractive Renaissance centre. And the town is surrounded by the largest palm forest in Europe —planted by the Arabs almost a thousand

BENEATH THE SEA

The Costa Blanca is at its most peaceful beneath the waves. Some of the best sites are around the Penyal d'Ifach rock. Underwater, its flanks are pocked with caves and swim-throughs, covered with anemones and sea urchins. Fish life is abundant as the Penyal is protected underwater too. Groupers and cow bream and even the occasional barracuda are common sights.

From top: Guadalest shrine; Hopital Real, Jativa; Alicante; Santa Maria, Huerto del Cura, Elche

years ago. At its heart is the flower-filled Huerta del Cura formal garden, criss-crossed by shady pathways and cooled by fountains.

In the Hills

The flatlands behind the Costa Blanca sharply rise to steep mountains swathed in maquis and remnant forest and broken by weatherworn rock faces—many of them topped by ruined Moorish castles. Semi-wilderness areas like the pine-covered Sierra de Espuña in Murcia and the hills around Alcoy and Cocentaina behind Benidorm offer wonderful nature walking, breathtaking views of the coast and the chance to spot threatened or endangered birds and mammals. Wild boar, barbary sheep and ibex are fairly common sights as are magnificent royal owls and royal eagles. Most tourists stay on the coast and visit the mountains, but it is equally easy to do the opposite and wake to the dawn chorus rather than the sputter of mopeds and the toots of horns.

The Coast

Even Benidorm's beaches can be peaceful. Just after dawn—when the light is at its most beautiful and the sea is a gentle mirror—the sand is deserted. This is the best time for a swim. By breakfast time it can be a struggle to find a quiet stretch of sand anywhere. The best options are the Cabo de la Não and the grassy covered coastal hills, cliffs and sheltered bays in the national park in Calblanque just south of Cabo de Palos in Murcia, both of which are relatively quiet outside the peak season.

From top: Huerto del Cura; Mula; Plaza Santa Domingo, Murcia; Calblanque; Benidorm

BAROQUE WORKS

Many of the Costa Blanca's serene churches are replete with baroque carving. The region's most famous sculptor was Francisco Salzillo (1707–83) who founded the so-called Murcian School of Sculpture and whose sculpture adorns the façade of Murcia cathedral. His naturalistic style remains influential today. There is a small museum devoted to Salzillo in Murcia (www.museosalzillo.es).

Shopping

While no one comes to the Costa Blanca to shop, some of the smaller towns preserve handicraft traditions and Alicante and Murcia cities are good places to stock up on food and wine and Spanish fashion.

Alicante
The region's capital offers the broadest range of shops. The streets west of Plaza Calvo Sotelo are full of Spanish clothing boutiques, and those around the foot of Castle Hill have artier shops. Alicante's Esplanada street market has shops and stalls selling everything from ceramics and jewellery to clothing and groceries. It is busiest on summer early evenings. More mainstream options include branches of the El Corte Inglés department store.

Wine
The best growing areas are the Rioja (which is famous for its earthy reds) and Ribera del Duero (which produces Spain's most expensive wines). Bottles from other regions include Priorato, Penedes (home of Torres wines) and Valdepeñas and the sherry-producing areas around Jerez in the south are well worth exploring. On the Costa Blanca, only Yecla near Alicante has one fine producer—Castaño. Spain categorizes wines as follows: Crianzas are two years old, with at least 12 months spent in cask; Reservas are three years old with at least one year in cask; and the finest, Gran Reservas, are five years old with at least two in cask.

From top: Altea; market stall; wines of the region; pottery on sale outside a workshop

---

TOTANA POTTERY

Artisans in the Murcian town of Totana have been firing pottery since Moorish times and their work is famous throughout Spain. Many still use traditional Arab tosta kilns where pots stand on a heated floor. Totana pots range from vast urns to smaller bowls and plates and are sold throughout the Costa Blanca. But they are cheapest and available in the greatest variety in Totana itself— which lies on the edge of the Sierra da Espuña and is easily reached along the E15 from Murcia.

With its mix of international and Spanish resorts, traditional towns and provincial mountain villages, the Costa Blanca has a diverse and varied nightlife.

Benidorm offers British variety show acts and thumping state-of-the-art dance clubs. Alicante has a lively, outdoor bar and café scene, live classical music and jazz and a Spanish club scene. And with its floodlit cathedral and celebrated tapas, Murcia is a great city to wander around at night.

Like a Local
For the best of the Spanish nightlife go out on the town in Alicante or Murcia. Alicante is liveliest and the best area is the Casco Antigo, especially on a weekend night. After 9pm this labyrinth of tiny streets buzzes with busy tapas bars that are heaving until first light. The Teatro Principal offers live performances from classical music to flamenco. Murcia's nightlife is focused on the tapas bars in the floodlit old centre.

Home from Home
Benidorm is the Costa Blanca resort town that never sleeps. And although it offers the greatest variety of ways to stay up all night most are non-Spanish. From around 9pm you'll find everything British and Irish here from pub quizzes and bingo to variety shows, live music, comedians, sports bars and pubs and huge dance clubs with big-name DJs. There are themed Spanish shows too—like the cabaret at the Benidorm palace but even these are conducted in English.

FESTIVALS

No one knows how to let their hair down like the Spanish, and the liveliest of all nights out are during the numerous regional fiestas—like the fiery Hogueras de San Juan in Alicante (midsummer night), Moros y Cristianos in Alcoy (▷ 52) and the Semana Santa celebrations in Mula (▷ 89).

There is plenty to do at night, from clubs to bars, restaurants and tapas bars

Eating Out

There's a wealth of restaurant choice on the Costa Blanca from traditional Spanish and Valencian paellas and fresh seafood dishes to pizzerias, curry houses, cafés serving all-day British breakfast and take-aways selling fish and chips.

Where to Eat
For the best choice head for Benidorm and its adjacent resorts. Here you can eat excellent Valencian or Spanish cooking in restaurants like La Palmera (▷ 82), or if you prefer to eat British, dine out at one of myriad British and Irish restaurants and pubs that pack the streets behind Playa Levante. Alicante and Murcia are far more Spanish—with the bulk of the best restaurants in the old parts of town around the castle and cathedral respectively. And there are some excellent rustic chic haute cuisine restaurants away from the coast—most notably in Játiva and Moratalla.

Types of Restaurant
Restaurants range from simple cafés offering thick espressos and *cafés con leche* (lattes) with a *bocadillo* (sandwich) to tapas bars, modest buffet eateries and more formal establishments staffed by waiters in black tie. Tapas are quintessentially Spanish. These little snacks were originally served on plates small enough to fit as a lid or *tapa* on a glass of beer. All tapas bars serve their own dishes and Murcia is famous throughout Spain for the diversity and idiosyncrasy of its tapas. Valencia and Murcia provinces both have their own regional cooking styles—the former strong on fresh seafood and the latter on fresh, crisp vegetables.

MEAL TIMES

The Spanish eat late, with breakfast (*desayuno*) between 9 and 10, lunch (*almuerzo*)—which is the main meal of the day—from 2 to 4 and dinner (*cena*) from any time after 9pm. Northern European restaurants around Benidorm keep to more British hours.

Dining options range from small tapas bars and beachside eateries to fine-dining in hotel restaurants

Restaurants by Cuisine

Although the provinces have their own cuisines, which should be sampled, restaurants throughout the region also serve Spanish and northern European food.

BRITISH/INDIAN

Everest Tandoori (▷ 81)
Himalaya (▷ 81)

CAFÉS/ICE CREAM

Bodega Galiana (▷ 47)
Café D'Or (▷ 47)
Deldado (▷ 104)
Europa (▷ 48)
Gori (▷ 48)

INTERNATIONAL

Auberge de France (▷ 47)
Internacional (▷ 81)
Tiffany's (▷ 82)
Tutti Frutti Pizzeria (▷ 82)
Los Zapatos (▷ 82)

SEAFOOD

Batiste (▷ 47)
Cabo Roig (▷ 47)
El Cigarralejo (▷ 104)
La Ereta (▷ 47)
El Granaino (▷ 48)
Los Habaneros (▷ 104)
Marenostrum (▷ 105)

El Molino (▷ 82)
Tiffany's (▷ 82)
La Veleta (▷ 105)
Virgen del Mar (▷ 105)

SPANISH/MEDITERANEAN

L'Albufera/Casa Paco Nadal (▷ 81)
Asador Ilicitano (▷ 47)
Batiste (▷ 47)
Las Cadenas (▷ 104)
Dársena (▷ 47)
La Ereta (▷ 47)
El Olivar (▷ 105)
El Pi del Senyoret (▷ 82)
El Pulpo Pirata (▷ 82)
Restaurante El Parador (▷ 105)
La Taberna (▷ 48)
Viva España (▷ 82)

SPANISH: REGIONAL

Acuario (▷ 104)
La Agelma (▷ 81)
Casa Cándido (▷ 104)
Casa Elias (▷ 47)
Casa Patricio (▷ 81)

El Churra (▷ 104)
El Granaino (▷ 48)
Hispano (▷ 104)
L'Hort (▷ 81)
La Huertanica (▷ 104)
Jumillano (▷ 48)
One One (▷ 48)
La Palmera (▷ 82)
Pintxa Kalea–Basque (▷ 48)
El Poblet (▷ 82)
Raimundo (▷ 105)
La Sidrería Escondida–Asuturias (▷ 48)
Venta La Magdalena (▷ 105)
Virgen del Mar (▷ 105)

TAPAS

L'Albufera/Casa Paco Nadal (▷ 81)
Bodega Galiana (▷ 47)
La Buena Tapa (▷ 104)
Il Cavacici (▷ 81)
El Molino (▷ 82)
El Pulpo Pirata (▷ 82)
La Veleta (▷ 105)
Los Zagales (▷ 105)

If You Like...

However you'd like to spend your time on the Costa Blanca, these ideas should help you tailor a perfect visit.

STYLISH HOTELS

Stay at Real De Faula (▷ 112), a mock hacienda beachside luxury hotel.
Mont Sant (▷ 111) is nestled under Jativa's Castillo.
Hotel L'Estacio is a gorgeous rural retreat (▷ 111).

FINE DINING

El Olivar (▷ 105)—for prize-winning gourmet local cooking.
La Agelma (▷ 81)—try their superb Valencian cooking.
La Ereta (▷ 47)—for modern cooking with a view.

MUSEUMS AND GALLERIES

MARQ (▷ 26–27) brings history to life.
Museo de la Asegurada (▷ 25) has works by Miró, Dalí and Picasso.
Casa-Museo Modernista (▷ 37) is the place to see Gaudiesque art nouveau.

KEEPING TO A BUDGET

On the beach: sunbathe and swim on one of myriad beaches.
Off the beaten track: stay in a little village and hike in the hills.
Festivals: visit the festivals—there's no entry charge (▷ 114).
Museums: many are free or have weekly free entry days.

Top to bottom: Hotels at Mar Menor; stained-glass windows in a restaurant in Elche; MARQ museum; the coastline near Benidorm
Opposite top to bottom: try horse-riding; clubbing on the Costa Blanca; alfresco dining in Murcia

HAVING FUN WITH THE KIDS

Terra Mítica (▷ 80) is the Costa Blanca's biggest theme park.

Visit Mundomar (▷ 80) for the aquaria, dolphins and sea life.

Pony treks—take a horse ride along the beach or up into the hills.

DANCE CLUBS

Westside (▷ 45), Alicante's busiest club, is packed with local students.

Penélope (▷ 80) is the biggest and most popular of Benidorm's dance clubs.

KM (▷ 79) plays host to some of Spain and the UK's top DJs in high season.

At Café Havana (▷ 44) you can learn to salsa with Latin Americans.

BARS AND TAPAS

Murcia's city centre (▷ 90–91) has the best and greatest variety of tapas in the region.

Visit Alicante's Casco Antigo (▷ 24) whose tiny whitewashed streets are filled with tapas bars.

Benidorm's old town (▷ 55) offers a taste of what you'll find beyond the big resort.

BEACHES

Benidorm (▷ 56) has twin bays of powdery white sand backed by a labyrinth of relentless neon-lit entertainment.

Calblanque (▷ 86–87) has coves, clifftop walks and flower-filled meadows.

Calpe (▷ 58)—a sweeping bay lapped by gentle waves and watched over by the towering Peñón de Ifach monolith.

SLEEPY VILLAGES

Mula (▷ 89) has sleepy winding cobbles watched over by a dramatic clifftop castle.
Guadalest (▷ 64–65) is a ruined fortress village perched on craggy peaks near Benidorm.
Cocentaina (▷ 70) is a tranquil hill town with a beautiful Renaissance centre.

CASTLES AND PALACES

Játiva's Castillo (▷ 68–69) is one of the largest and best preserved in southern Spain.
Alicante's Castillo de Santa Barbara (▷ 28–29) offers superb views.
Gandia's Palau Ducal (▷ 62–63) is an example of imperial Spanish splendour and a former home to the Borgias.

CHURCHES AND MONASTERIES

Visit Murcia's cathedral (▷ 92–93) to see a vast and imposing fusion of baroque, Renaissance and neoclassical.
Orihuela's cathedral (▷ 36) hides lavish baroque splendour behind a modest exterior.
Orihuela's Colégio de Santo Domingo (▷ 35) is the Escorial of the east.
Elche's basilica (▷ 30) offers superb views from the bell tower.

UNSPOILED NATURE

The Peñón de Ifach (▷ 58–59) has wildflower meadows, craggy rocks and wonderful diving.
Illa de Tabarca (▷ 32–33) offers some of the best diving and snorkelling in the eastern Mediterranean.
Sierra de Espuña (▷ 94–95) is a series of pine-covered mountains cut by walking trails and soared over by eagles and vultures.

Top to bottom: Guadalest valley; ruined Moorish fortress in Guadalest; Orihuela; Murcia's cathedral

Costa Blanca by Area

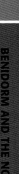

ALICANTE AND AROUND

BENIDORM AND THE NORTH

MURCIA

The Costa Blanca's most interesting coastal city has an imposing Moorish castle, lively restaurants and nightlife and good museums. A string of elegant Renaissance towns and villages lies in its hinterland.

Sights	24–40
Walk	41
Shopping	43
Entertainment and Activities	44–45
Restaurants	47–48

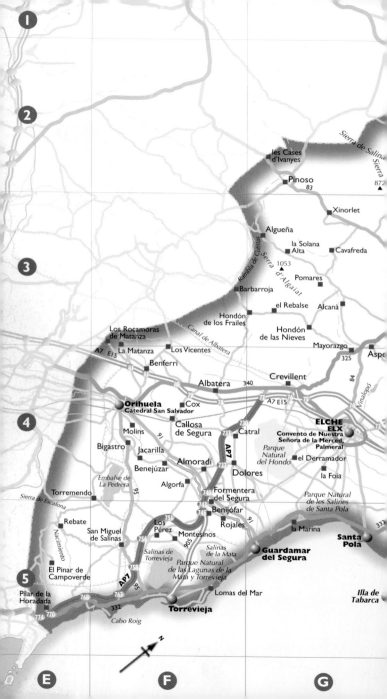

344

A31

Sierra de la Solana

Cabezo
de la Virgen

81

Las Virtudes

Serra de la Serreta

Las Ventas

Villena

la Solana

81

Cañada

Beneixama

Galeno

el Bovar

Salinas

La Peña
Rubia

Biar

Les
Fontanelles

Banyeres
de Mariola

Umbría

Sax

Serra de l'Arguenya

1228

80

A31

Mossén
Joan

Onil

Castalla

Parque Natural
del Carrascal de la
Font Roja

Elda

Serra de Maigmó

Verde

Petrer

onovar
onòver

Ibi

A36

Mola

Torrosella

Novelda
Casa Museo Modernista,
Santuario de Santa
María Magdalena

la
Sarganella

Serra de la
Penya Roja
1226

340

Tibi

Monforte
del Cid

Escanelia

Maigmó

Casa de la
Cuesta

A36

Agost

Alecua

la Torre de
les Maçanes

Urito

Serra Mitjana

Montnegre

Jijona
Xixona

Serratella

l'Alcoraia

A31

Pla de
l'Olivera Alta

Coves de
Canalobre

Montnegre

Vall-longa

San Vicente
del Raspeig

340

Preventorio

Bacarot

A7 E15 70 65

Tangel

Busot

Aigües

Torrellano
Bajo

77 340

71

Mutxamel

AP7 E15

ALICANTE
ALACANT

la Santa
Faç

67

el Campello

332

eroport
Alacant
l'Altet

Castillo de Santa Bárbara,
Museo Arqueológico

Sant Joan
d'Alacant

Urbanova

l'Albufereta

Cap de
Santa Pola

Cap de les Hortes

C o s t a

B l a n c a

0   10 km

0   5 miles

H   J

Alicante

HIGHLIGHTS

- The Concatedral de San Nicolás de Bari
- The old Moorish streets of the Casco Antigo
- The Iglesia de Santa Maria
- The castle (▷ 28–29)
- MARQ (▷ 26–27)
- Museo de la Asegurada
- The Town Hall

This port town is the region's hub. It's prosperity and large student population give it a great restaurant and nightlife scene and it's the Costa Blanca's most resolutely Spanish coastal town.

Settlement Alicante has a long and distinguished history. It was first settled by the Phoenicians, who established a trading post here, and later by the Greeks, Romans, Carthaginians and Iberians. But like so many in southern Spain the city grew most markedly under the Moors. They left their mark on the city by expanding the castle (▷ 28–29) and building the Casco Antiguo—a maze of tiny white-washed and flower-filled streets that make up the neighbourhoods of Santa Cruz and San Roque. They are wonderful to lose yourself in—on the way to the castle or while in search of a bar.

Clockwise from left: The colourful tiled façade of a house in Alicante; Playa de Postiguet near Alicante province; Explanada de España, a quiet residential street; the clocktower of the Ayuntamiento

Links to the past In 1248 the city was re-conquered by the Castilian king Alfonso X and by 1308 belonged to the fledgling kingdom of Valencia. Parts of Iglesia de Santa Maria date from this period. Other handsome buildings in the old centre include the bulky 17th-century Concatedral de San Nicolás de Bari, with a Renaissance façade and a splendid baroque interior and the twin-towered 18th-century Ayuntamiento (town hall), a late baroque building with a glorious entrance hall.

Today The city has some fine museums. The Archaeological Museum (MARQ ▷ 26–27) is the best historical museum on the Costa Blanca. And the Museo de la Asegurada preserves an important collection of Spanish and international 20th-century art—including pieces by Miró, Dalí and Picasso—in a restored Renaissance grain house.

THE BASICS

H4

🍽 Restaurants in the Casco Antiguo and La Ereta on castle hill (▷ 48)

💶 Churches, Museo de la Asegurada and Castillo free; MARQ moderate

ℹ️ Avenida Rambla Mendez Nuñez 23, Alicante, tel 965 20 00 00; Calle Portugal, 17 bajo, tel 965 92 98 02

🚉 Major international airport; trains from Alicante north and South

Alicante: Museo Arqueológico

- The medieval gallery
- Former hospital building
- State-of-the-art audiovisual displays
- Models of archaeological sites

TIP

- For quiet visits avoid weekends and come when it first opens.

When it gets too hot to walk the streets or even lie in the sun head for this award-winning, air-conditioned museum for a glimpse of Alicante's long and distinguished history.

Award-winning The Museo Arqueológico, or MARQ, is housed in the former hospital of San Juan de Dios near the waterfront. The museum holds some 81,000 items, but is perhaps most remarkable for its modern, engaging interactive and audio-visual displays—which earned it the European Museum Award in 2004.

The galleries The collection is divided into five principal chronological sections: Prehistory, Iberian, Roman, Medieval and Modern. Each section offers a window into the plethora of peoples and

Clockwise from left: Middle Ages Room; medieval archaeological remains; the Roman culture room

cultures that shaped Alicante. The displays are punctuated with sound effects—the clank and hubbub of a medieval street, the serenade of Moorish troubadours and interactive displays. Little annexes show films depicting aspects of historical life from Stone Age artisan work to pottery-making. The medieval gallery, which is perhaps the most captivating, covers the city's Islamic period—the longest of any. It shows Alicante as a vibrant cosmopolitan centre bustling with Muslims, Jews and Christians, and it showcases some beautiful plain and coloured ceramics.

Take the children The museum also features excellent re-creations of archaeological sites, including a shipwreck complete with amphorae, which, together with the interactive displays, is popular with children.

THE BASICS

www.marqalicante.com
+ H4
✉ Plaza Dr. Gómez Ulla s/n, Alicante
☎ 965 14 90 00 (information; 945 14 90 06 (tickets)
🕐 Jul–Aug 11–2, 6–midnight; Sep–Jun Tue–Sat 10am–7pm; Sun 10–2. Hours might vary annually
🍽 None
♿ Good
💰 Moderate

Alicante: Castillo de Santa Bárbara

HIGHLIGHTS

- Views
- Battlements and Moorish tower
- Eduardo Capa collection
- The walk up the hill from the city centre

TIP

- There is a shady little open-air café just left of the main gate as you enter the castle. It has views equally as wonderful as those from the battlements.

This imposing castle perched high on a hill serves as a constant reminder of the city's Islamic heritage and its bloody past. The views from the battlements are among the best in the Costa Blanca.

Saint's day The castle was built in the late 9th century by the Moors who ruled much of Iberia from AD711. They were ousted from Alicante by the Alfonso the Wise on 4 December 1248, the saint day of St. Barbara. The castle was named in her honour. Alfonso further fortified the original Muslim battlements, beginning around the castle's highest point—the only portion of the original Moorish building to survive. The castle was impregnable until the War of the Spanish Succession at the turn of the 16th century. Then it fell to the English and subsequently the French

Clockwise from far left: Exploring the castle; a mosaic of a medieval knight guards a doorway in the castle; inside the castle complex; visitors pause to take in the view; details of a coat of arms on the castle walls; looking over Alicante from the castle

after relentless bombardment from the sea and a huge booby trap mine. It was occupied once more by the English during the Peninsular War against Napoleon. The English-built battlements remain to this day. The castle served as a state prison in the early 20th century before retiring from active service to become a tourist attraction in 1963.

Highlights The building retains only a smattering of its original decorative features, including occasional *mudejar* flourishes. But it houses the largest collection of modern and contemporary Spanish sculpture in the world. There are more than 700 pieces on display, dating from the late 19th century, 250 of which are part of a permanent collection. They include Salvador Dalí's *Newton* together with work by Benlliure, Capuz, Orduna, Alberto Sánchez, Manolo Hugué and Los Oteiza.

THE BASICS

www.alicante.es/ingles/culture/museos-santabarbara.html

✛ H4

✉ Monte Benecantil, Alicante

☎ 965 16 21 28

🕐 Apr–Sep daily 10–8; Oct–Mar daily 9–7. Elevator operates at these times

🍴 Restaurant and café

♿ None

🎫 Castle free; lift inexpensive

Elche

The Moorish fortress (left); palm trees (middle); Santa Maria, Huerta del Cura (right)

THE BASICS

www.turismedelx.com

🔲 G4

🖐 Castle and museum: moderate; basílica: free; basílica tower: moderate

📞 Plaça de Parc 3, tel 966 65 81 95

HIGHLIGHTS

● Palmeral and Gardens (▷ 31)
● Basílica de Santa Marta.
● Archaeological museum and castle
● Misteri d'Elx festival
● Dama de Elche sculpture

TIP

● Elche is a city of views and the best are from the castle walls and the tower of the Basílica de Santa Marta.

With its tracts of towering date palms, baking sun and semi-desert surrounds, Elche feels as North African as it does Spanish. It is the only city in Spain with two UNESCO World Heritage attractions.

Don't miss Most tourists to Elche (Elx) visit only to see the Palmeral botanical gardens and miss the city itself. It's easy to see why: Elche's hinterlands are a sprawl of warehouses and shoe factories. But at their heart is the Villa Murada—a maze of little streets next to the river and crowded around the massive walls of the castle and the towers and cupolas of the Renaissance Basílica de Santa Maria. Although many of the historical buildings in the Villa Murada date from the Renaissance the street plan is entirely Arabic and a handful of the original Muslim buildings remain. Most notable are the Banys Arabs (Arab bathhouse) and La Calaforra, a hulking rampart that formed part of the fortifications of Islamic Elche. Views from the castle ramparts and church tower are superb.

City museum Start an exploration at the slick, modern city museum, which traces Elche's history through a series of informative audio-visual displays, reconstructions and showcases of objects.

Cultural event On 14 and 15 August every year the city celebrates the Misteri d'Elx Festival —a sung, medieval pageant that celebrates the Assumption of St. Mary, Jesus's mother, to Heaven. It is a UNESCO Intangible Cultural Heritage (ICH) event.

Huerto del Cura Hotel (left); a fountain in the grounds of Huerto del Cura (right)

TOP 25

Elche: Palmeral

Elche's Palmeral is a vast forest of date palms planted by the Arabs. They still form the largest palm forest in Europe. This is enclosed within a park and includes little lakes and formal gardens.

Moorish legacy The Palmeral is the only extant example of Arab agricultural practices to have survived in modern Europe and is a UNESCO World Heritage Site. Large, planted palm groves are typical features of the North African landscape and were brought to Iberia during the Islamic era. Elche's was planted in the Almoravid era—Muslim Spain's cultural zenith—in the 10th century. Almost all of the Iberian peninsula was part of the Arab empire at this time and the forest was one of a series of grand civic and architectural projects overseen by the rulers. It is an engineering feat, involving the diversion of water through elaborate irrigation channels to produce an artificial oasis.

Gardening priest At the heart of the Palmeral is the Huerto del Cura—The Vicar's Garden—a formal Arabic garden dotted with little lily ponds and florid with temperate and tropical flowers. It was named in honour of Don José Castaño, an 19th-century Catholic prison chaplain who devoted his life to administering and remodelling the gardens and baptizing and naming the palms. The Palmeral and Huerto del Cura gardens hide a series of buildings and monuments including a number of traditional rural houses, a small museum, sculptures and a tiny faux-baroque chapel preserving the remains of Juan Orts Román, the Huerto's last caretaker.

THE BASICS

✠ G4

☎ 966 65 81 95; Huerto del Cura: 965 45 19 36

🕐 Daily 10–5; Huerto del Cura: Mar–Oct daily 10–9; Nov–Feb daily 10–6

🍴 Restaurant

&. Good

💷 Huerto del Cura moderate

HIGHLIGHTS

- Original irrigation canals
- Huerto del Cura
- Imperial date palm
- Cactus Garden
- Heliconias and bird of paradise flowers

TIP

- The Palmeral and Huerto are very popular. Come early or late in the day when the coach parties and heat have abated, and avoid weekends.

ALICANTE AND AROUND

★ **TOP 25**

Illa de Tabarca

HIGHLIGHTS

- Marine reserve
- Genoese fortifications and church of Nueva Tabarca
- Boat crossing from Santa Pola

TIP

- Tabarca is easy to visit. Companies in Alicante, Benidorm or the small resort town of Santa Pola all tout day trips. Hotel concierges and tourist offices can put you in touch.

This craggy, bone-dry archipelago set in aquamarine waters just south of Alicante is now a marine reserve—with some of the best snorkelling in the Spanish Mediterranean.

History In medieval times, Tabarca was known as the Isla de Sant Pau (Saint Paul's Island) as it was widely believed that the evangelist was shipwrecked here. It became part of the Republic of Genoa before falling to the Arabs and then being reconquered by Spain. In 1768 King Carlos of Spain gave sanctuary here to a group of Genoese expelled from the Tunisian island of Tabarca, who built the current port town, the fortifications and the splendid and bizarrely proportioned church. The settlers called their new home Nueva Tabarca. Tabarca's permanent population is around 50,

Tabarca, south of Alicante, was fortified in the 18th century. Today it offers excellent snorkelling possibilities

making it Spain's tiniest populated island. Tourists outnumber locals by as much as 50 to 1 in the high season.

Today The islands are one of the best places in Spain for diving and snorkelling. The Mediterranean accounts for just 0.8 per cent of the world's oceans yet it accounts for 7.5 per cent of all described marine species. And the Western Mediterranean is its richest area. Despite this, snorkelling or diving on the Costa Blanca can be a frustrating experience. Marine life has been decimated by over-fishing, pollution and contamination from ballast water. Tabarca and its surrounding rocky islets have been protected since 1986 and offer a glimpse of the sea's extant richness. The best snorkelling is around the smaller islands, away from the port, and over the artificial reef.

HIGHLIGHTS

● Nuestra Señora de
Monserrate church
● Santa Iglesia Catedral de
San Salvador de Orihuela
(▷ 36)
● Palácio del Marqués de
Rubaclava
● Colégio e Iglesia de Santo
Domingo

TIP

● Be here in the late afternoon when the sun turns
Orihuela's stone a deep
burnished gold.

**Orihuela is the best-preserved
Renaissance town in the lowlands of the
Costa Blanca. And despite its beauty and
proximity to Alicante it remains free of
big tour parties for most of the year.**

Explore The town invites aimless wandering—
past the honey-coloured churches and majestic
civic buildings and through the little fountain-filled
plazas. At every turn there's a charming view, of
the sierra that rises steep in arid green behind
the town, or of a church spire set against a deep
blue sky. The centre is home to some of the most
important Renaissance buildings on the Costa
Blanca. These include the 18th-century neoclassical church of Nuestra Señora de Monserrate.
The church is dedicated to the town's patron saint,
Our Lady of Montserrat, whose effigy is carried

Colegio de Santo Domingo (left); bell-tower of the Colegio (middle); the carved portal at the entrance to the Colegio (right);

around the city during the colourful Procesión de la Patrona festival in September. Just along the street is the Iglesia de Santiago built in the 15th century over an original Visigoth church, then converted into a mosque before reverting to a church after the Christian Reconquest. The Isabeline-Gothic church door, La Portada Principal, preserves some eye-catching Muslim decorative features and there's an enchanting late Gothic chapel inside.

Grand buildings Orihuela is as much a city of palaces as churches. The tourist office is housed within the Palácio del Marqués de Rubaclava—an early 20th-century neo-baroque mansion. A little further to the east is the grand Colégio e Iglesia de Santo Domingo, a complex of monastic and ecclesiastical buildings nicknamed the 'Escorial of the East' after the famous royal palace in Madrid.

THE BASICS

www.orihuelaturistica.es

➕ F4

🍴 Restaurants and cafés

✋ Castle and museum expensive; basílica free; basílica tower inexpensive

ℹ️ Palácio del Marqués de Rubaclava, Calle Francisco Díe 25, Orihuela, tel 965 30 27 47

35

Orihuela: Catedral de San Salvador

TOP 25

The richly carved and ornate interior of the cathedral

THE BASICS

www.orihuelaturistica.es

🔼 F4

✉ Plaza Teniente Linares

🕐 Sacred Art Museum Mon–Fri 10.30–1.30, 4–6.30, Sat 10–1.30

🍴 Restaurants and cafés nearby

♿ Adequate

🎟 Free; Sacred Art Museum inexpensive

HIGHLIGHTS

● Cadenas door
● Sacred Art Museum
● Soaring Gothic arches
● Velázquez's *Temptation of St. Thomas Aquinas*

TIP

● Avoid weekends and come early or late in the day to appreciate the church's prayerful serenity.

Orihuela is the Costa Blanca's most opulent and best-preserved Renaissance town and this magnificent Gothic cathedral is the jewel in its crown.

Venture inside The Cathedral of Christ the Saviour was built in the 14th century, utilizing material from the Al Jama mosque that the Spanish destroyed in the Reconquest. With its squat tower, thick walls and Romanesque façade, the cathedral looks plain and even a little ungainly. But the interior is a magnificent, if stark, interplay of lines, curves and sacred space which reaches its climax in a series of ethereally light, soaring Gothic vaults, whose intersections are crowned with exquisitely carved floral medallions. Behind the cathedral are tranquil colonnaded cloisters.

Mudejar The cathedral is one of the few buildings in the region with marked Mudejar touches. The Mudejar is at its most marked in the Cadenas—one of three principal entrances to the cathedral—which is Gothic in shape but entirely Arabic in its sculpted adornments. The Loreto gate is crowned by an ascending panoply of saints and is in the Gothic style, and the 16th-century Anunciación gate is late Spanish Renaissance with a profusion of early baroque flourishes.

Excellent art The church's sacred art museum is one of the most distinguished on the Costa Blanca and houses paintings by Ribera, Salzillo and a highly regarded Velázquez, *The Temptation of St. Thomas Aquinas*.

Novelda: Casa-Museo Modernista

The celebrated art nouveau interior of the townhouse

This fastidiously restored townhouse a short drive from Benidorm or Alicante preserves one of the finest art nouveau interiors in Southern Spain.

Leading architect The house's modest and neoclassical exterior is unimpressive. But its interior is magnificent. Both were designed and built between 1903 and 1906 by the Murcian Pedro Cerdán Martínez, a contemporary of Gaudí, and the Costa Blanca's foremost decorative architect from the end of the 19th century until the Belle Époque. He was also responsible for Murcia's famous Casino (▷ 103).

Elaborate details Like Gaudí, Cerdán was interested in the play between artificial and natural geometrical shapes. This is especially apparent in his decorative use of wood, fine stone and stained glass. The lobby and upper floors are connected via a marble staircase that curves upward like the interior of a seashell. Vinous wooden panels that interlock like plates on a turtle's carapace line its ascent, together with a twisting, vine-like banister. Two elaborate stained-glass skylights decorated with swirling, diaphanous and multi-hued floral patterns light the reception area and the stairwell. The rooms are no less ostentatious. The study is a riot of elaborately carved hardwood and undulating panels; the ballroom a heady swirl of scarlet and gilt over a mock-mudejar tiled floor; and one of the bathrooms contains a giant tub, hewn from a single, cyclopean slab of Italian marble.

THE BASICS

www.novelda.es

⊞ G3

✉ Calle Mayor 24, Novelda

☎ 965 60 02 37

🕐 Mon–Fri 9–2, 4–7, Sat–Sun 11–2, 5–7

♿ None

🎟 Free

HIGHLIGHTS

● Twin stained-glass skylights
● Ballroom
● Marble bathrooms
● Elaborately carved woodwork in the study

More to See

BIAR

www.biar.es

This tiny fortified town is dominated by an impregnable Moorish castle which withstood a sustained attack and prolonged siege before finally falling to Jaime I in 1245. With its steep cobbles, quiet little plazas and paucity of visiting tourists, the town feels timeless and very Spanish. There are great views out over the terracotta roofs, sierra and surrounding plain from the Castillo itself. The Renaissance church of Nuestra Señora de la Asuncion has a superb, intricately carved plateresque door.

➕ H2 ✉ 55km (34 miles) west of Alicante ☎ Castillo de Biar: 965 81 03 74 🕓 Castillo de Biar: Tue–Fri 10–2, Sat 10–2, 4–6, Sun 10–2 🍴 Restaurants and cafés 🚌 From Alicante

CUEVAS DE CANALOBRE

www.cuevasdecanelobre.com

The limestone hills immediately to the north of Alicante are a honeycomb of caves and tunnels, many of them encrusted with dripping stalactites and towering stalagmites. The Cuevas de Canalobre, which take their name from an elaborate, lacy, candelabra-shaped flowstone that encrusts the main cave, are one of the few cave systems to be lit and formally open to the public. And they showcase some of the largest chambers in Spain.

➕ J4 ✉ Near Busot, 24km (15 miles) north of Alicante ☎ 96 569 92 50 🕓 Jul to mid-Sep daily 10.30–7.30; mid-Sep to Jun Mon–Fri 10.30–4.50, Sat–Sun 10.30–5.50 🍴 Refreshments ♿ Fair ✋ Moderate

ELCHE: CONVENTO DE NUESTRA SEÑORA DE LA MERCED

Although this convent is nominally one of the oldest Christian buildings on the Costa Blanca, being founded by the Sisters of Mercy in the early Renaissance, shortly after the Reconquest. However it was extensively renovated in the 18th and 19th centuries in a 17th-century Renaissance style that matches much of the rest of Elche's old centre.

Stalactites and stalagmites in the Cuevas de Canalobre

There is a beautiful Gothic/early Renaissance chapel at its heart, together with remains of the 12th-century Arab bath house that occupied the site in Moorish times.
🔶 G4 ✉ Passeig de Santa Llucía, Elche ☎ Tue–Sat 10–1, 4.30–8.30, Sun 10–1 🍴 Cafés and restaurants ✋ Free

GUARDAMAR DEL SEGURA
www.guardamar.net
Tourism is smaller-scale at this burgeoning Spanish beach town surrounded by pretty beaches and set in sand dunes just south of Alicante. The town's castle and 13th-century church and little archaeological museum attest to its long and distinguished history. It was founded by the Iberians and then occupied by the Romans before becoming a Moorish port.
🔶 G5 ✉ 40km (25 miles) south of Alicante; Museo Arqueológico y Etnológico, Casa de Cultura, Colón 60 ⏰ Museum: Mon–Fri 9–2, 5–8.30 ✋ Inexpensive 🍴 Restaurants and cafés 🚌 From Alicante, ferry to Tabarca, (Cruceros Tabarda tel: 966 70 21 22)

JIJONA
www.jijona.com
Spain's famous *turron*—nougat made of almond and honey—comes from this town nestled in the sierra behind Alicante. It is still made by hand by some 30 small family businesses in the area and the town has a small museum devoted to the confection.
🔶 J4 ✉ 28km (17 miles) north of Alicante 🍴 Restaurants and cafés 🚌 From Alicante
Museo del Turron
✉ Calle de Vicente Cabrera, Jijona ☎ 965 61 02 25 ✋ Free

MONOVAR
This town set in lush vineyards is the Costa Blanca's foremost producer of wine. The strong Monsatrel grape reds contrast with the delicate, light rosés, and the sweet Fondillon dessert wines. Tasting is available at the Bodega Salvador Poveda.
🔶 G3 ✉ 40km (25 miles) west of Alicante 🍴 Restaurants and cafés 🚌 From Alicante

Old beach houses at Guardamar de Segura

Vineyards at Monovar

NOVELDA: SANTUARIO DE SANTA MARIA MAGDALENA CHURCH

This quirky art nouveau church encrusted with *azulejo* mosaic and sitting sentinel on a little hill was designed by local architect José Sala Sala who was strongly influenced by Antoni Gaudí. The building recalls the Sagrada Familia, but was built between 1918 and 1946. It has a unique urn shape.

✚ G3 ✉ 30km (18 miles) west of Alicante 🍴 Cafés and restaurants

SANTA POLA

www.turismosantapola.es

This family resort town and busy port hosts one the largest fishing fleets in Spain and ferries leave from here to the Tabarca islands (▷ 32–33). There are plenty of hotels and restaurants, long, broad, sandy beaches to the north and south and a squat 16th-century castle with good views.

✚ G5 ✉ 18km (11 miles) south of Alicante 🍴 Cafés and restaurants 🚌 From Alicante ✋ Castle free

SAX

www.sax.es

Sax preserves one of the most dramatically situated of all Costa Blanca castles, perched eyrie-like on a craggy ridge and beautifully lit at night. Sax itself sprawls down the hillside into the steep Vinalopó valley. The main tower is Moorish but the courtyards and keep are from a later period.

✚ H3 ✉ 45km (28 miles) west of Alicante ☎ Tourist office: 965 47 40 06 🍴 Cafés and restaurants

TORREVIEJA

www.torrevieja.com

This popular beach resort provides a family-orientated alternative to Benidorm and the beaches of the north. There is a big music festival here in August and the natural parks on the nearby Torrevieja and La Mata salt flats are important sanctuaries for coastal birds, with some 250 resident and migratory species.

✚ F5 ✉ 48km (30 miles) south of Alicante 🍴 Cafés and restaurants 🚌 From Alicante via Elche ⛴ Ferry to Illa de Tabarca

The church at Novelda, heavily influenced by Gaudí

The castle dominates Sax

Walk to the Castle

Alicante's Castillo de Santa Barbara offers sweeping views. There are shady areas at the summit offering respite from the heat.

DISTANCE: 2km (1.6 miles)   **ALLOW:** 2–3 hours with stops

START

PROMENADE
✚ e4   🚌 S, G, M

1 Begin on the coast at the eastern end of Alicante's palm-lined, dragons' tooth beach promenade–the Esplanada de España at the junction of the broad Rambla de Mendez Nuñez.

2 Walk 400m (436 yards) inland and a block east to the towering domes of the Concatedral de San Nicolas (▷ 25)–the city's largest and most impressive church.

3 Walk a block south east to the Plaza de Ayuntamiento for a quick visit to the Town Hall, one of the city's most striking baroque buildings.

4 Then head east along Calle de Jorge Juan and up the steps to the Plaza Santa Maria and Alicante's oldest church (▷ 25). The Museo de la Asegurada next door houses the finest collection of modernist Spanish paintings in the region.

END

CASTILLO
✚ f4   🚌 E2, 50

7 After a long cold drink explore the castle's ramparts and the paintings and sculptures that are dotted around the castle before heading back to Alicante via the castle lift and Postiguet beach.

6 Walk to the Plaza de Cuartel–a broad quad at the centre of the building watched over by the massive former barracks. There is a small exhibition space inside and a café restaurant with wonderful views nearby.

5 Head northeast out of the Plaza climbing steeply through the white-washed narrow streets and following the signs for the castle. You will cut through the landscaped gardens of the Parque Monte Benacantil and the Parque de la Ereta, which has a little waterfall and a pretty bridge, before winding your way to the main gate of the castle.

Shopping

BODEGA SELECCIÓN
www.bodegaseleccion.com
A huge choice of Riojas, Ribera del Dueros and local regional bottles alongside wines from the rest of Europe and an excellent choice from Argentina and Chile.
✚ c5 ✉ Calle Italia 4, Alicante ☎ 965 92 17 38

EL CORTE INGLÉS
www.elcorteingles.es
Spain's largest department store chain sells everything from Spanish books to household items, fashion and a great choice of Spanish CDs. There is an excellent air-conditioned restaurant on the third floor.
✚ c4 ✉ Avenida Maisonnave 53, Alicante ☎ 965 92 50 01

ESPLANADA MARKET
Stalls and shops bustle with activity at this evening market, which offers everything from bric-à-brac to fashion, foodstuffs and arts and crafts.
✚ d4 ✉ Esplanada de España, Alicante

FRAN HOLUBA
A good and high-quality choice of ceramics, leather, small homeware items and artefacts.
✚ d1 ✉ Calle Jaime Segarra 16, Alicante ☎ 965 24 45 95

LLCORERIA BERNARDINO
The best selection of Spanish and imported wines in Alicante with more than 2,500 Spanish vintages, the largest choice of which are from La Rioja.
✚ a5 (fold-out map) ✉ Calle Alberola 38, Alicante ☎ 965 28 08 73

MANGO
Great shoes, slinkily cut clothing in a range of bright colours for 20–40-something women, and a very popular house perfume, all at good prices.
✚ c4 ✉ Plaza Calvo Sotelo 12, Alicante ☎ 965 21 89 02

MERCADO CENTRAL
A bustling street market crammed with fruit and vegetables from all over the region together with freshly caught fish and other market groceries.
✚ d3 ✉ Avenida de Alfonso el Sabio, Alicante ☎ None

MARKETS
In Spain, Mercado Municipal markets sells foodstuffs and operate on a daily basis. Mercadillos work weekly and sell arts, crafts and bric-à-brac. Both take place in the heart of any Spanish town and are good for picking up the basics for a picnic or a few souvenirs. There are also *mercadillos artesano*, usually on a Sunday morning, entirely devoted to arts and crafts. Tourist offices and the better hotels can provide details of where to find them.

PATRACOL
www.patracol.com
Tasteful beautifully crafted notebooks, diaries, cards and paper items, unusual children's toys, hand-made photo albums and, should you get lost at sea in your way to the Illa de Tabarca, astrolabes.
✚ d4 ✉ Calle Castaños 25, Alicante ☎ 965 20 79 40

PEDRO SORIANO
Beautiful modern secular sculpture in a range of materials including white and dark wood.
✚ Off map at b1 (fold-out map) ✉ Plaza San Antonio 2 ☎ 965 20 78 54

SHIRTCITY.ES
www.shirtcity.es
This online, Alicante-based, shirt company allows you to design your own personalized or branded T-shirts complete with self-designed logo, picture or inscription. Shirts can be sent ahead to your hotel or posted back to the UK by the company as a present.

ZARA
www.zara.com
A popular Spanish boutique with a broad range of fashionable clothes at decent prices. Although there are some items for men and children, most of the clothing is for women.
✚ c4 ✉ Avenida Maisonnave 42, Alicante ☎ 965 92 37 41

Entertainment and Activities

BAO BAR
On a recent visit, anatomically sculpted leather suits were dangling above the long mahogany bar and the eclectic crowd twirling on the blood-red moulded bar were sipping ice-cold Amstel and chatting over chill-out jazz. Local artists supply the wall décor.
✚ e4 ✉ Calle Labradores 11, Alicante ☎ None ⏰ Daily evenings only

BASIC SQUARE
This no-frills, very Spanish student bar decorated with local photographic art attracts a lively young crowd and lives up to its name—the drinks menu consists of cheap beer and little else.
✚ e4 ✉ Plaza San Cristóbal 7, Alicante ☎ None ⏰ Daily evenings only

CAFÉ HAVANA
A little slice of Hispanic America in Alicante, attracting people of all ages from the city's Hispanic American population and offering salsa dancing on Monday nights.
✚ d4 ✉ Calle Rambla de Méndez Núñez 22, Alicante ☎ 965 21 69 26 ⏰ Daily evenings only

CANÍBAL
www.canibalshop.com
A lively gay-friendly pub-style bar near the castle which is a popular start-of-the-evening weekend spot from around 10pm.

✚ d4 ✉ Calle Cesar Elguezebal 26, Alicante ☎ 965 20 25 23 ⏰ Closed Sun

EL CARIBE
Lovers of Hispanic American dance from salsa and rumba to merengue will enjoy this lively club that is packed with local Hispanic Americans at the weekends. There are free dance classes some nights.
✚ d4 ✉ Calle General Primo de Ribera 14, Alicante ☎ 965 20 77 85 ⏰ Tue–Thu 8.30pm–3am, Fri–Sat 10.30pm–4.30am

CELESTIAL COPAS
Live and DJ-driven flamenco, bossa nova and boleros, an eclectic crowd and off-the-wall art and décor on the walls.
✚ d4 ✉ Calle San Pascoal 1, Alicante ☎ None

DESAFINADO
A popular student dance

<table>
<tr><td>WATERSPORTS</td></tr>
</table>

Watersports dominate on the Costa Blanca. The larger resorts offer diving (best around Tabarca island), water-skiing, and wind and kite surfing (Tarifa in Andalucia is the best location in Europe for both). Whilst snorkelling is decent off any rocky area far from the busy beaches, the Mediterranean is heavily overfished and sea life is richest off the protected Tabarca island.

bar named in honour of the Tom Jobim bossa nova track but playing more standard euro-club sounds well into the next morning.
✚ d3 ✉ Calle Santo Tomas 6, Alicante ☎ None

DESDEN
Even in the depths of the low season this bar buzzes with local life. Students and locals flock here for some of the cheapest beer in town. The best spot to watch the action is from the upstairs gallery tables that look out over the long red bar and the thronging crowd that spills out onto the street. Hispanic hip hop and contemporary flamenco from the likes of Almas Rebeldes play over the sound system.
✚ e4 ✉ Calle Labradores 22, Alicante ☎ None ⏰ Daily evenings only

DIVINE CLUB
www.divineclub.net
This is a large, very popular 20-something club with pop on Thursday and a mix of European club sounds, house and hip hop at weekends from resident DJ Juan Cruz. Full itinerary and a map of how to reach the club is on their website.
✚ G4 ✉ Doctor Caro 14, Elche ☎ None

LA LLUM
An alternative to Desden —crammed with an eclectic crowd of people

from students to tourists who drink draft and bottled beer and a tiny dance floor that pounds until the latest of the early hours.

⊞ d4 ⊠ Calle Montengonat Padre Maltés, Alicante ☎ None

PACHÁ

www.pachatorrevieja.com
The Costa Blanca outpost of this vast Ibiza club chain. The music is hard house, hip hop and European club sounds, and the crowd young, fit, alcohol-fuelled and scantily clad. Booms until well after dawn in high season only.

⊞ Off map at F5 ⊠ Delfina Viudes, Torrevieja ☎ 965 70 48 78

PIANO BAR

A traditional piano and cocktail bar with comfy armchairs and a cigar and brandy crowd of 40 and over.

⊞ e4 ⊠ Hotel Melia, Plaza Puerta del Mar 6, Alicante ☎ 965 20 50 00

EL RACO DE MAMA LOLA

This is one of Elche's most popular start-of-the-evening tapas bars, serving local beer and wine together with a range of great tapas, including cold meat plates like *solomillo al hojaldre* and seafood. Busy after 9pm.

⊞ G4 ⊠ Calle de Alfredo Mira Gran 1, Elche ☎ No phone

STEREO

www.salastereo.com
The dance club of choice for the Alicante indie scene and local rock and rollers.

⊞ Off map at d1 ⊠ Calle Pintor Velázquez 5, Alicante ☎ 966 35 86 41 ◷ Daily, evenings

TEATRO CIRCO

The city's premier concert venue is housed in a pretty Edwardian theatre in the centre and offers a range of different shows from drama to live classical popular and world music, ballet and jazz.

⊞ Off map at F4 ⊠ Plaza Poeta Sansano, Orihuela ☎ 966 74 01 04 ◷ None

TEATRO PRINCIPAL

www.teatroprincipaldealicante.com
Ballet, contemporary music played by performers from Paco de Lucia to Dulce Pontes, circus shows from the likes of

---

CINEMA

There are cinemas in Benidorm, Alicante, Javea, Alfaz del Pi and Torrevieja. Some screenings show English-language films with Spanish subtitles. The acronyms VO (*versión original*), VOS (*versión original subtitulada*) are indicative—written beside the listing. www.info-costablanca.com lists all the cinemas with phone numbers.

---

the Shanghai Circus, serious drama and classical music and jazz in a tastefully restored neoclassical theatre in the centre of the city.

⊞ d4 ⊠ Plaza Ruperto Chapí 7, Alicante ☎ 965 20 31 00 ◷ Daily

EL VERMELL CASA DE VIÑOS

An eclectic crowd of all ages come to this arty little bar lost in the huddle of Moorish streets below the castle. It's a true wine bar—selling little more than a wide choice of Spanish bottles and strong coffee.

⊞ e4 ⊠ 8 Calle Argensola, Alicante ☎ None ◷ Mon–Sat evenings only, closed Sun

WESTSIDE

Alicante has far more students than tourists. And this hip-hop and reggae bar serving mojitos and piña coladas is one of their favourite hang-outs, making it popular even out of season.

⊞ e4 ⊠ Calle Labradores 3, Alicante ☎ None ◷ Daily evenings only

Z KLUB

www.zklub.net
One of the city's plushest and more traditional dance clubs and one of the few with a door policy. The music is hip hop and club and the crowd 20- and 30-something.

⊞ d4 ⊠ Calle Coloma 3, Bajos Casino, Alicante ☎ None ◷ Evenings only

Restaurants

PRICES

Prices are approximate, based on a 3-course meal for one person.

€€€   over €40
€€   €20–€40
€   under €20

ASADOR ILICITANO (€€)
www.asadorilicitano.com
Castilian fare served in a rustic restaurant with generous cuts of meat, hearty roasts and fish dishes.
🚩 G4 🖂 Calle Maestro Giner 9, Elche ☎ 965 43 58 64 🕓 Daily lunch and dinner. Closed Sun and 15–30 Aug

AUBERGE DE FRANCE (€€€)
French haute cuisine served in a beautiful villa set in a pine and palm tree garden. Specialties include the ultra-light *bacalao en soufflé de ajos tiernos* (cod and garlic soufflé).
🚩 Off map at f4 (fold-out map) 🖂 Calle Flora de España 32, Alicante ☎ 965 26 06 02 🕓 Tue–Sun 1pm–4pm, 8pm–11pm

BATISTE (€)
One of the town's most popular rice and seafood restaurants.
🚩 G5 🖂 Pérez de Ojeda s/n, Santa Pola ☎ 965 41 14 85 🕓 Daily lunch and dinner

BODEGA GALIANA (€)
www.bodegasgaliana.com
A convenient lunch spot situated directly between the castle and the cathedral, offering over 15 kinds of tapas, cuts of fresh cured ham, Spanish cheese, lunches and ice cold juices and draught Mahou beer. Very good value breakfasts served until late.
🚩 G4 🖂 Plaza de Congreso Eucarístico 10, Elche ☎ 96 545 63 53 🕓 Daily breakfast, lunch and dinner

CABO ROIG (€–€€)
This excellent seafood restaurant lies in the port area, nestled under the imposing Renaissance fort near the Torre Vigía tower. There are Mediterranean views, excellent fresh fish and one of the largest selection of wines in Valencia province.
🚩 F4 🖂 Urb. Cabo Roig, Orihuela ☎ 966 76 02 90 🕓 Daily lunch and dinner

EATING SPANISH
With the advent of multi-awarded haute cuisine restaurants like El Bulí on the Costa Brava, Spanish cuisine is gaining international aplomb to rival that of France. Cooking is strong on seafood and meat and makes use of very fresh ingredients. Spanish cured meats like *jamón Serrano* and cheeses like manchego are as good as any in Europe and are popular tapas–accompanied by a glass of red wine or sherry *(jerez)*.

CAFÉ D'OR (€)
This lovely café run by an elderly couple has a long marble bar, huge streetside windows, great coffee and ice-cold draught Amstel.
🚩 d4 🖂 Calle San Francisco 61, Alicante ☎ 965 14 42 50 🕓 Mon–Sat 7.30–2.30pm. Closed Sun

CASA ELIAS (€€)
Traditional Valencian home-cooking with excellent rice and vegetable options.
🚩 G3 🖂 Rosales 7, Cinorlet, Monovar ☎ 965 95 97 17 🕓 Thu–Tue lunch only

DÁRSENA (€€€)
www.darsena.com
There are some 200 different kinds of rice dishes—including various paellas—in this enormous boat-shaped restaurant in Alicante's dock area.
🚩 Off map at G5 🖂 Marina Deportiva, Muelle de Levante 6, Alicante ☎ 965 20 75 89 🕓 Mon–Sat 7.30–2.30pm

LA ERETA (€€€)
This beautiful glass-fronted Modernist space is situated in a little rock garden just below the castle. It offers fine dining with some of the best views on the Costa Blanca—out over Alicante town and the Mediterranean.
🚩 e3 🖂 Parque de la Ereta, Alicante ☎ 965 14 32 50 🕓 Summer: Tue–Sat lunch and dinner; winter: Tue–Wed 2–4pm; Thu–Sat 2–4, 9–11pm

EUROPA (€)

Home-cooked simple food served in a modest but conveniently located restaurant in the centre of town. Busy at lunchtime.
🛉 F4 ✉ Plaza Europa, Orihuela ☎ 966 74 26 78 🕐 Mon–Sat lunch and dinner. Closed Sun and Aug

GORI (€)

Spaniards and tourists come to this little outdoor plaza café to eat an inexpensive alfresco breakfast or light lunch accompanied by excellent strong *café con leche*.
🛉 d4 ✉ Pintor Lorenzo Casanova 5, Alicante ☎ 965 14 42 50 🕐 Mon–Sat 7.45–late. Closed Sun

EL GRANAINO (€€€)

The well-established fine-dining restaurant in Elche serves a variety of food from a huge menu and is particularly renowned for its seafood and regional specialties. Excellent wine list with some unusual Valencian bottles.
🛉 G4 ✉ Calle Josep Maria Buck 40, Elche ☎ 966 66 40 80 🕐 Daily 9.30–4pm, 7.30–midnight

JUMILLANO (€€€)

www.restaurantejumillano.com
One of Alicante's longest established restaurants with a menu of carefully prepared and beautifully cooked local dishes.
🛉 d4 ✉ Calle César Elguezábal 62, Alicante ☎ 965 21 29 64 🕐 Mon–Sat dinner. Closed Sun

ONE ONE (€€)

A real community restaurant with a cast of regulars who dine on the dishes of the day—there's no formal menu and listen to tales of the owner, Bartoleme's travels around Spain and Latin America. Photos adorn the walls and the house wine and beer flows readily.
🛉 d4 ✉ Calle Valdes 9, Alicante ☎ 965 20 63 99 🕐 Daily lunch and dinner

PINTXA KALEA (€€)

Basque specialties like bullock fillet steak, cod and *chuleton* (chops) are beautifully prepared

FORTIFIED WINES

Spain is famous for its *jerez* wines or sherries. Sherry-making techniques were probably brought across from Shiraz in Iran (which lent its name to the Spanish town and the drink–*Sherish* in Arabic). The wines are graded according to strength and consistency as follows: fino is the driest and palest and includes a variety called manzanilla. Amontillado is darker and longer aged. Oloroso (or 'fragrant' in Spanish) is older, darker and richer still. And sweet or cream sherry (*jerez dulce*) is made by sweetening one of the above varieties with Pedro Ximénez or Moscatel wine.

and served on vast white plates in this smart, open-plan modernist space. Lively chat comes with a backdrop of bossa nova electronica and Ibiza chillout.
🛉 e4 ✉ Plaza San Cristóbal 11, Alicante ☎ 965 14 58 41 🕐 Summer: daily lunch and dinner; Winter: Tue–Wed 2–4pm; Thu–Sat 2–4, 9–11pm

LA SIDRERÍA ESCONDIDA (€)

www.lasidreiaescondida.com
Tapas at this popular Asturias restaurant near the hill leading to the castle include scorpion fish pasties, wild boar chorizos, ostrich salami and 13 different Spanish cheeses—try the blue-goat's milk cabrales with a full-bodied Ribera del Duero red.
🛉 e4 ✉ Plaza San Cristóbal 8, Alicante ☎ 965 20 31 93 🕐 Daily lunch and dinner

LA TABERNA (€€)

The most popular choice for meat and paella-lovers on this busy, restaurant and bar-filled pedestrian street under the shadow of the castle. There are good tapas too, including *gambas ajillo* (garlic prawns), *calamare romana* (fried squid) and *patatas bravas*.
🛉 e4 ✉ Calle Labradores 24, Alicante ☎ 615 66 78 95 🕐 Daily lunch and dinner

Benidorm and the North

Benidorm and its adjacent resorts may not be sophisticated but they promise all year round sunshine and the liveliest nights in the Mediterranean at a bargain price. For peace and quiet and something more Spanish head inland to the sierra and its pretty little mountain towns.

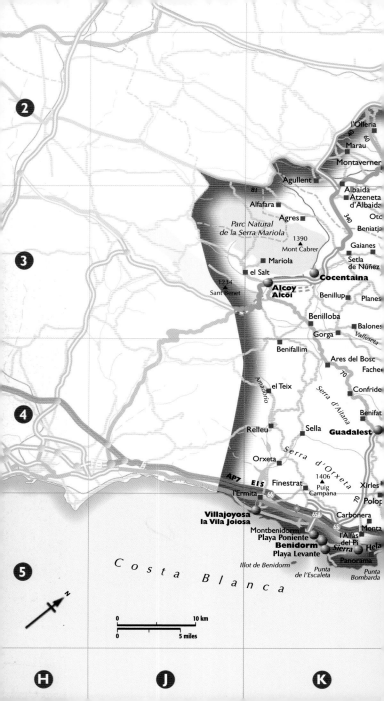

2

3

4

5

l'Olleria

Marau

Montaverner

Agullent

81

Albaida
Atzeneta
d'Albaida

Alfafara

Agres

Oto

Beniatja

340

Parc Natural
de la Serra Mariola

1390
Mont Cabrer

Gaianes

Setla
de Núñez

Mariola

el Salt

Cocentaina

1234
Sant Benet

Alcoy
Alcoi

Benillup

Planes

Benilloba

Balones

Gorga

Valleseta

Benifallim

Ares del Bosc

Fache

70

el Teix

Serra d'Aitana

Confride

Benifat

Relleu

Sella

Guadalest

Amadorio

Orxeta

Serra d'Orxeta

Xirles

AP7

Els

Finestrat

1406
Puig
Campana

Polop

l'Ermita

66

Carbonera

Monta

65A

Villajoyosa
la Vila Joiosa

65

l'Alfàs
del Pi

Hela

Montbenidorm

Playa Poniente

Benidorm

Playa Levante

Sierra

Panorama

Illot de Benidorm

Costa Blanca

Punta
de l'Escaleta

Punta
Bombarda

N

0   10 km

0   5 miles

H

J

K

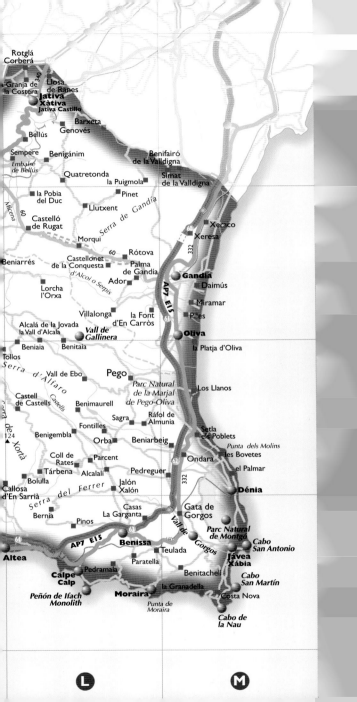

Rotglá
Corberá
la Granja de
la Costera
Llosa
de Ranes
Játiva
Xàtiva
Játiva Castillo
Barxeta
Genovés
Bellús
Sempere
Benigánim
Embalse
de Bellús
Quatretonda
la Puigmola
Pinet
la Pobla
del Duc
Llutxent
Castelló
de Rugat
Morqui
Rótova
Castellonet
de la Conquesta
Palma
de Gandía
Ador
Lorcha
l'Orxa
Villalonga
la Font
d'En Carròs
Alcalá de la Jovada
la Vall d'Alcala
Vall de
Gallinera
Beniaia
Benitaia
Tollos
Serra
d'Alfaro
Vall de Ebo
Pego
Castell
de Castells
Benimaurell
Sagra
Ráfol de
Almunia
Fontilles
Benigembla
Orba
Beniarbeig
Coll de
Rates
Parcent
Tárbena
Alcalalí
Pedreguer
Bolulla
Jalón
Xalón
Callosa
d'En Sarrià
Serra del Ferrer
Casas
La Garganta
Bernia
Pinos
Altea
AP7 E15
Benissa
Teulada
Calpe
Calp
Pedramala
Paratella
Peñón de Ifach
Monolith
Moraira
la Granadella
Punta de
Moraira

Benifairó
de la Valldigna
Simat
de la Valldigna
Serra de Gandía
Xeraco
Xeresa
332
Gandía
Daimús
Miramar
Piles
Oliva
la Platja d'Oliva
AP7 E15
Parc Natural
de la Marjal
de Pego-Oliva
Los Llanos
Setla
ele Poblets
Punta dels Molins
les Bovetes
Ondara
el Palmar
332
Dénia
Gata de
Gorgos
Vall de Gorgos
Parc Natural
de Montgó
Cabo
San Antonio
Jávea
Xàbia
Benitachell
Cabo
San Martín
Costa Nova
Cabo de
la Nau

L   **M**

Alcoy

Carved stonework (left); Plaça de Dins (middle); the city skyline (right)

THE BASICS

➕ K3

ℹ️ Sant Lorenç 2, tel 965 53 71 55; Mon–Fri 9.30am–8pm, Sat 10–1.30, 4.30–7.30, Sun 10–1.30

HIGHLIGHTS

● Renaissance centre
● Art nouveau Circulo Industrial cultural centre
● Moors and Christians festival

TIP

● Try to visit in late April to experience the Moros y Cristianos festival.

The inland city of Alcoy, nestled in a steep valley between the Molonar and Barchell rivers, is one of the most resolutely Spanish large towns in the region. Its annual Moros y Cristianos pageant is spectacular.

Growth Alcoy was a sleepy semi-medieval village until it rapidly expanded and grew wealthy with the Spanish industrial revolution. Some of Iberia's first steam trains ran from here to the coast, and the town remains a centre of the Spanish textile and lace-making industries. The heart of the city is a mix of Renaissance and art nouveau. It is well worth a visit—wandering between the shady plazas and Moorish alleys and the broad 19th-century avenues lined with prosperous shops. Of the city's interesting buildings the finest are the 18th-century baroque Santa Maria church in the heart of the Renaissance old town and the art nouveau decoration in the Circulo Industrial cultural centre.

Festival Most visitors come to Alcoy for the elaborate, costumed festival (22–24 April) celebrating the Reconquest of the Moors under Al Azraq by the crusader Spanish captained by King Jaime I. For three days locals dress up as knights in armour, Moorish princesses, Berbers, Basque mercenaries, kings, queens and courtiers and parade through the streets to the sound of fireworks and brass bands. The culmination is a mock battle when the town, captured by the victorious Moors, is reconquered by Christian knights inspired by the heavenly apparition of King George.

Altea

One of Altea's narrow,
stepped streets (left);
La Virgen de Consuelo
church (right)

Altea is like a mini, low-rise Benidorm, backed by a pretty Moorish town and tends to be popular with families and retired holiday-makers. And, like Benidorm it boasts more than 3,000 hours of sun each year.

Haunt of artists In the early 20th century paint-ers like Genaro Palau and Joaquin Mompo came to Altea to paint the town—itself and on canvas. They left murals and wall paintings throughout Altea and depictions of its pretty, winding, white-washed Moorish streets clustered around the blue terracotta dome of La Virgen de Consuelo church in front of a wall of steep, maquis-covered hills. Imitations of their work fill Altea's galleries.

Holiday centre The once tranquil village is now crowded in by big roads and a wall of hotels and restaurants that stretch along the seafront for kilometres. Artists and artisans increasingly sell rather predictable work to tourists. But gems can still be found in the streets around church, espe-cially Calle Mayor, which are packed with little boutiques. A handful of Palau's original murals are preserved on the streets and in private houses. And the town has a quirky museum, the Museo Étnico de la Música, tucked away in a stately town house in the old centre and showcasing more than 400 instruments lovingly collected by ex-pat Uruguayan local Carlos Blanco Fadol. Altea's beach is some 3km (2 miles) long and is backed by an attractive, palm-shaded promenade watched over by numerous shops, hotels and restaurants.

THE BASICS

www.alteadigital.com

➕ K5

ℹ Calle Sant Pere, tel 965 84 41 14; Mon–Fri 9.30–2, 5–7.30, Sat 10–1

Museo Étnico de la Música
www.museomusicaetnica.com

✉ Palau Altea s/n

☎ 966 88 19 24

🕐 Daily 9–5

💶 Inexpensive

HIGHLIGHTS

● La Virgen de Consuelo church
● Early 20th-century street art
● Museo Étnico de la Música
● Shops on Calle Mayor

TIPS

● Avoid swimming at the beach's eastern end, where there is a sewage outlet.
● Nightlife is lively.

Benidorm Town

PLAÇA
DE LA
SENYORIA

HIGHLIGHTS

● Beaches
● Vibrant nightlife
● Old Moorish fishing village
● Iglesia San Jaime

TIP

● Book a last-minute package holiday over the internet to get the best Benidorm deals.

In the 50 years since it began to be developed as a resort, Benidorm town has grown from a tiny fishing village to a mini-city backed with towering high-rises and visited by some 4 million people every year. Many love it so much that they choose to settle.

Popular resort The secret to the resort's success is its unpretentious, simple recipe. Benidorm offers the holiday equivalent of supermarket shopping. It is not sophisticated. Nor does it try to be. But it does offer sun and mass-market fun at a cut price. The resort's benign microclimate guarantees more than 3,000 hours of sun every year. And its placid waters mean that swimming offshore is safe for everyone from toddlers to pensioners. Carefully planned service means that visitors who struggle

Clockwise from far left: A quiet moment in the town; the exterior of San Jaime church; a central plaza with souvenir stalls; Plaça de la Senyora

with foreign menus and languages will find that they never have to eat or speak differently from how they do at home. And the huge wealth of entertainment from karaoke to cabaret is invariably in English, Dutch or German.

Look under the surface Even tourists looking for a more authentically Spanish holiday are drawn to Benidorm—especially those on a budget. If you book ahead, nowhere in Spain offers comfortable rooms at a better price and the resort is within easy driving distance of all the Costa Blanca's sights. And hidden within the streets of the faux English pubs and Danish cafés there is still an old Moorish fishing town with little white streets, the charming Renaissance village church of San Jaime and a handful of authentically Spanish restaurants and bodegas.

THE BASICS

www.benidorm.org

🟊 K5

ℹ️ Avenida Martínez Alejos 16, tel 965 85 13 11; Mon–Fri 9.30–8, Sat 10–1.30, 4.30–7.30, Sun 10–1.30

Benidorm: Beaches

Coast near Benidorm (left); Playa de Levante (right); Benidorm town (opposite)

THE BASICS

www.benidorm.org

✚ K5

HIGHLIGHTS

● Sunrise on the beaches
● Sunbathing in the early morning
● Promenade restaurants
● Watersports on Playa Levante
● Sunset walks along the esplanade
● Views from the church of San Jaime

TIP

● The beaches are at their best very early in the day.

Benidorm became the Mediterranean's most developed resort for one reason alone—its beaches. And while they are far from being the havens of solitude and unspoiled natural beauty they were until the 1960s they still remain some of the finest in Spain.

Two beaches The resort is made up of twin long and half moon beaches separated by a rocky promontory. The eastern and most developed beach, Playa Levante, is a 3km (2-mile) broad strand of white-pepper fine sand backed by a palm-shaded and paved promenade. It is also the busiest beach in the Mediterranean. Playa Poniente is a little quieter and shorter. It is also backed by a promenade and it has a little port at its eastern end. The tallest and plushest of the beachfront hotels lie here.

Beach days begin early The sun rises deep yellow-red from the inky Mediterranean just after 6am in summer (at 7am in winter). Yet before 8am the beaches are almost deserted, making this an enchanting time of the day. The middle of the day is the best time to escape the heat with some watersports, a tour or a long, relaxed lunch in one of the myriad restaurants-with-a-view behind the promenade. In the early evening, the beach begins to empty and the promenade fills with tourists strolling up to the church of San Jaime on the promontory, to watch the shadows lengthen and turn Benidorm a rich golden yellow. Sunsets can be as late as 9.45pm in high summer.

Calpe and the Peñón de Ifach Monolith

HIGHLIGHTS

● Views of the Peñón de Ifach
● Climbing the monolith

TIPS

● Set off very early to beat the heat on the Peñón walk and to catch the best light.
● Bring a snorkel and mask on your Peñón walk–there is great underwater life around the rock.

No resort on the Costa Blanca has a more breathtaking setting than Calpe's, squeezed between the towering Peñón de Ifach monolith and the slopes of the sierra, and fronted by glorious beaches.

Development Calpe has long basked in the beauty of the Cyclopean Peñón de Ifach monolith that rises almost sheer from the sea to dominate the skyline for miles around. And it's long grown rich on its fame. In Roman times locals ostensibly claimed that Hercules visited here to try his strength on the boulder. More recently it's estate agents who are carving up the steep hillsides above the town—into tiny plots with a view—sold to hordes searching for their place in the sun. The Peñón also gave the town its name—both 'Calpe' and 'Peñón' translate prosaically as 'rock' from

From far left: Plaça de Mariners (top); Calpe on Playe de Levante (bottom); the mono-lith dominates the horizon; painted stone steps lead through narrow streets

Phoenician and Spanish respectively. And shelter from the rock has given Calpe a gentle harbour, a broad, long crescent beach and a large and constant stream of visitors from nearby Benidorm.

The monolith It's still possible to escape the crowds and have the monolith's magnificence almost to oneself. Leave at dawn for its flanks with a large water bottle and some good walking shoes and allow an hour to climb to the summit. The trail leads through a tunnel in the bottom of the rock face before winding its way up the lower slopes for a vertiginous clamber to the top. The Peñón is a protected area and is home to numerous birds including the rare Audouin's gull and greater flamingoes on the adjacent salt flats. Some 300 species of wild flowers burst into colour on its slopes in spring.

THE BASICS

www.calpe.es

🕂 L5

✉ 20km (12 miles) north-east of Benidorm

🍴 Bars and restaurants

♿ Adequate

🎟 Free

ℹ Plaza del Mosquit, tel: 965 83 85 32

Dénia

TOP
25

HIGHLIGHTS

- Castle
- English cemetery
- Old fishing village
- Iglesia de Asunción

TIP

● Ferries to the Balearic islands, leave from here: Balearia Lines, Estación Marítima ☎ 902 16 01 80; www.balearia.com

This family resort town huddled around an impressive Moorish hilltop castle and flanked by beaches makes a good, more laid-back alternative to brasher Benidorm and its sister resorts to the south.

The past Dénia has a long and distinguished history. The city was inhabited by the Phoenicians in the first millennium BC and subsequently by the Greeks, the Romans (who named the city in honour of the goddess Diana), the Iberians and the Moors. The layout of what remains of the old town dates mostly from the Muslim Almoravid era and the Renaissance Christian Reconquest. The town had a large population of émigré British raisin traders in the 19th century. A few are buried in an abandoned and overgrown English cemetery behind Marineta Cassiana beach.

From left: Painted houses in the old fishing quarter; the harbour is dominated by the old fortress; the waterfront

Attractions The castle is most impressive. Entrance is through an imposing 12th-century Almoravid door beneath the massive walls of the Cos de Guardia tower. Inside there's a small Governor's Palace, a series of Renaissance court-yards and a modest archaeological museum tracing the town's past. Other buildings include the lovely 18th-century, baroque Iglesia de Asunción (Church of the Assumption) and a hud-dle of bright pastel-painted sugar-cube houses around the old docks. Ferries leave from here to the Balearic Islands.

Beaches Dénia has two very different beaches. There's good snorkelling in glassy-clear water off Les Rotes beach and a stretch of fine sandy beach at Marineta Cassiana lapped by a placid sea and backed by a tiled promenade.

THE BASICS

www.denia.net

M4

55km (34 miles) north of Benidorm

Restaurants

Poor

Castillo moderate

Tourist office, Plaza Oculista Buiges 9, tel: 966 42 23 67

Train from Benidorm and Alicante (irregular service

Gandia

**This very Spanish resort town makes a
good choice for those seeking a resort-
based holiday with an Iberian feel. And
the city is worth visiting for the magnificent Palau Ducal dels Borja palace.**

Old-fashioned Gandia is a Spanish beach resort
with long, broad beaches of powdery white sand
and attractive streets, some of which are lined with
mock hacienda and art deco buildings. It's the kind
of place where they still sell candyfloss by the sea
and have pony rides along the sand. And as relatively few foreigners make it here it's a great place
to eat local, speak local and meet a local.

Lavish palace Even those choosing not to stay
here should consider visiting the Palau Ducal
dels Borja palace—a palace once owned by the

From left: The interior coutryard at the Palacio Ducal; the sports habour; Gandia's beach

famously decadent Dukes of Borja (the Borgias)—in the 15th century and embellished with opulent baroque decoration in the 18th. The exterior is sober, but the interior is replete with florid gilt, exquisite wall and ceiling paintings and brilliant *azulejo* (coloured tiling). The most ostentatious room of all is the Galería Dourada—a cavernous 'Chinese box' of apartments, one leading into another, whose decoration is a kaleidoscope of gilt stucco, mosaic, mirrors and stately portraits.

Other attractions There are a few other sites of interest, including a 16th-century fort with an original Muslim tower to the north of the city in the Alqueiria del Duc neighbourhood, and the 15th-century Real Monasterio de Santa Cruz monastery which includes remains of the city's original fortified walls.

THE BASICS

www.palauducal.com

➕ M3

✉ Calle Duc Alfons el Vell, 1

☎ 962 87 14 65

🕐 Palau Ducal: Mon–Sat 10–2 3–7, Sun 10–2; guided tours at 11.30, 12.30 and 5.30

🍴 Restaurant

♿ Some

✋ Palau moderate

ℹ Avenida Marqués del Campo, tel: 962 87 77 88

Guadalest

HIGHLIGHTS

- Views out over the Guadalest valley to the coast
- Ruined castle
- Miniature whitewashed bell-tower
- Views of the town from the lower town
- Museo de Microminiatura

TIP

- The best views of the old town are from the road to Benidorm.

Even the coach loads that arrive by the dozen in high season cannot detract from the charm of this tiny hilltop fort town perched on a series of precipitous and crumbling rocks in the sierra above Benidorm.

Rocky perch Guadalest is the most dramatically situated of all the Moorish fortified towns that dot the mountains of inland Costa Blanca. Its crumbling, pocket-sized ramparts and the lacy bridges that link them appear so precariously balanced that they seem set to plunge into the valley below at any moment. Jaime of Aragon seized control of the original Moorish fort after a prolonged siege in the 13th century. And the castle he built in its place stood unblemished for over 500 years—withstanding an earthquake in 1644 and attacks

Clockwise from left: Guadalest entry gate and shrine; looking across the valley and back to the town; almond trees

by Charles, Duke of Habsburg during the Wars of the Spanish Succession before finally beginning to crumble after a further quake in 1748.

Two villages The town is made up of two settlements. The lower village is a handful of houses owned by locals and a greater number of tourist shops, restaurants and hotels run by them. There's a quirky little museum—devoted to all things miniature in this tiniest of towns—with everything from a nano-steam train to an Eiffel tower seen through magnifying glasses. The upper village contains the original fort, a ruined cemetery, the bell tower that has become the logo of the town and a smattering of other buildings and ruins. It is reached through the Puerta de San José—a tiny arch that leads through a tunnel hewn from the raw rock onto the cobbles of Old Guadalest.

THE BASICS

www.guadalest.es

✚ K4

✉ 28km (17 miles) north-west of Benidorm

☎ 965 88 52 98

🕐 Castle: Apr–Oct daily 10–8; Nov–Mar 10–6

🍴 Restaurants, bars and shops in the lower town

Museo de Microminiatura

✉ Calle Iglesia 5

☎ 965 88 50 62

🕐 Daily 10–9 (6 in winter)

✋ Moderate

Jativa

HIGHLIGHTS

● Basílica church of La Seu
● San Feliu church
● Renaissance centre
● Castle

The steep, narrow streets of this mountain town huddle below the castle in a maze of echoing cobbles and sunburned terracotta. They're lined with Renaissance buildings and ornate churches that attest to a distinguished past.

Religious influence Jativa has been of strategic and economic importance since pre-Roman times. The Romans and the Carthaginians built a fort here, the Iberians minted coins and the Moors introduced paper manufacture into Europe through the town. The Borja (or Borgia) dynasty were from Jativa, and the town has the dubious honour of having given the Catholic church two Borgia popes—most infamously Rodrigo Borja. Rodrigo became Pope Alexander VI through a Machiavellian mix of corruption, bribery, intrigue

A statue of Jativa-born artist, José de Ribera (left); looking across the town from the ramparts of El Castillo (middle); old town mansions (right)

and murder that has made his name legend more than five hundred years after his death. Although a Catholic priest, he was far from celibate—fathering at least four children, one of whom, Lucrezia, was his lover. Many of the Jativa's most opulent buildings were built with Borgia money, including much of the Basílica church of La Seu. Other buildings of note include the 15th-century and baroque Palácio del Marqués de Motortal and the 19th-century Casa de Diego.

Explore the town Jativa invites wandering and the best route is through the little fountain-filled plazas and streets that make-up the town centre to the San Feliu church on castle hill, an enchanting 13th-century Romanesque church filled with stunning Renaissance church art, and eventually to the castle itself.

THE BASICS

✛ L2

✉ 80km (50 miles) north of Alicante

🍴 Many small restaurants and the excellent Mont Sant on castle hill (▷ 111)

♿ Some

🚃 Trains from Alicante and Gandia via Alcoy

TIP

● Come in the late afternoon when the crowds have thinned and the warm golden light of the Iberian sun turns the walls a rich red brown.

With its rugged Moorish battlements and dramatic setting, this fortress looks like a setting for a story from the *Arabian Nights*. In moonlight it's easy to imagine flying carpets soaring from its ramparts.

Must-see If you visit only one castle in the Costa Blanca region make it this one. In Southern Spain, only Granada's Alhambra is more spectacular. The castle walls, palaces and Islamic gardens stretch for almost a kilometre (0.6 miles) along the spine of a long, high ridge above the labyrinthine Arab streets of Jativa town. There is a different, glorious 360-degree view out over the plain.

Castillo Like most of the Costa Blanca's castles Jativa's Castillo was built mainly by the Arabs, who linked an earlier fortification with their own larger

The view from the castle ramparts over the surrounding town and farmland (left); the huddle of buildings within the castle walls (right)

edifice. The older section is known as the Castillo Menor and it lies to the east, immediately inside the castle's Gothic gateway. Although it was largely built by the Romans, it became a Carthaginian and later an Iberian stronghold. Hannibal's wife, Himilce, is said to have given birth to a son here in AD 218 and gives her name to the main tower. The Moorish and Renaissance Spanish Castillo Mayor sits immediately above to the west, separated from the Castillo Menor by a large open quad. Buildings here include two beautiful chapels—the Capilla de San Jordi and the Capilla de Santa Maria, which houses the tombs of rulers of two medieval Spanish states, Mazmorra, Count of Urgell, and the last Count of Pallars. There are a series of beautiful Islamic gardens too, the patio de Celoquia (with Roman paving), a claustrophobic dungeon and some high Moorish watchtowers.

THE BASICS

➕ L2

✉ Carretera Castillo

☎ 962 27 42 74

🕐 Apr–Oct Tue–Sun 10–7; Oct–Mar Tue–Sun 10–6

🍴 Excellent restaurant at Hotel Mont Sant (▷ 111) in the castle grounds

♿ Adequate

💰 Moderate

❓ Occasional summer concerts

More to See

BENISSA

www.benissa.net

This pocket-sized terracotta town is a world away from the hustle and bustle of nearby Benidorm and makes an interesting stopover on the drive inland. It is as old Spanish as the coast is new rich, with stately town houses and civic buildings fronted by very Moorish doorways and windows covered with traditional *reja* shutters. Many line Calle Purisima—the town's central street, which leads up to the vast Catedral de la Marina. The town was founded by the Moors—its name is derived from the Arabic Beni Isa, or Isa's children, and refers to the people of the tribe who first settled here.

✚ L5 ✉ 26km (16 miles) from Benidorm 🍴 Restaurants and cafés 🚌 From Benidorm

CABO DE LA NAU

Craggy cliffs filled with nesting sea birds rise sharply from a limpid, deep blue Mediterranean to form this precipitous, rocky and scrub-covered cape at the easternmost point of the Costa Blanca. Although stretches near the road are covered with a proliferation of 'secluded' holiday villas lined up to admire the sea view it is still possible to escape the crowds on dusty paths near the waterfront, especially in the far south of the cape.

✚ M5 ✉ 50km (31 miles) east of Benidorm 🍴 Restaurants and cafés

CABO SAN MARTÍN

To escape the nearby crowded beaches and enjoy a spot of snorkelling in clear turquoise sea head to this rocky promontory at the southern end of Jávea Bay. A path leads here from the coastal road at the Cruz de Portichol—a roadside stone cross—through a lavender and maquis meadow offering enticing coastal views. Allow half a day to explore.

✚ M5 ✉ 50km (31 miles) east of Benidorm

COCENTAINA

www.cocentaina.es

Tourists are slowly beginning to

Isla de Portichol off the coast of Cabo San Martín

Palau Condal at Cocentaina

discover this delightful little Renaissance village with its untidy labyrinth of honey-coloured medieval buildings watched over by a Moorish tower sitting high on a rocky mount above the town. The highlight is the grand 13th-century Palau Comtal palace, a carefully restored fortified palace with a series of magnificent fully furnished Renaissance rooms. There's excellent walking in the near-by Sierra Mariola. The town makes a good base for the lively Moros y Cristianos festival in nearby Alcoy.

➕ K3 ✉ 60km (37 miles) west of Benidorm 🍴 Restaurants and cafés
🚌 From Alicante

Palau Comtal

✉ Plaza del Pla s/n ☎ 965 59 01 59
🕐 Mon–Fri 9.30–noon, 4–6 ✋ Inexpensive

JÁVEA

www.xabia.org

Jávea, which sits on a glorious bay enclosed by the rocky capes of the Cabo de la Nau and Cabo San Antônio (▷ 73) is said to be the sunniest place on the Costa Blanca.

Its handsome Renaissance centre attests to the long, glorious history the town had before it became one of the coast's most popular family resorts. Fine houses and mansions line the streets that cluster around the Gothic church of San Bartolomé on the Plaza de la Iglesia. An interesting little archaeological museum housed in a stately palace tells Jávea's story from pre-Roman times through the Moorish period and the Reconquest.

➕ M5 ✉ 55km (34 miles) north of Benidorm 🍴 Restaurants and cafés
🚌 From Benidorm

MORAIRA

What was once a fishing village with colourful bobbing boats is now the Puerto Banus of the Costa Blanca—a low-key rural city of whitewashed holi-day homes and sky-blue swimming pools climbing into the pine forests in the hills and watching out over the marina and the Mediterranean. The coastline is crowded, but it remains lovely, the newsagents stock more copies of the *Telegraph* than *The Sun*

The buildings of Moraira behind the modern marina

Jávea's Plaza de la Iglesia

★

and the restaurants and services are the best in the region.

⊞ L5 ✉ 35km (22 miles) north of Benidorm 🍴 Restaurants and cafés 🚌 From Benidorm

OLIVA

www.tourist-oliva.com/en/

This family resort still feels a little like a Spanish fishing village—and for now it remains a relatively peaceful harbour in the sea of high-rises and condominiums that has washed over the Costa Blanca. There are long and broad beaches just outside the town lapped by a child-friendly, gentle sea and the old town centre has some fine Renaissance buildings, along with some decent hotels and restaurants.

⊞ M3 ✉ 42km (26 miles) north of Benidorm 🍴 Restaurants and cafés

PARC NATURAL DE MONTGÓ AND THE CABO SAN ANTONIO

This 2,000ha (4,940-acre) park offers a glimpse of how the Costa Blanca looked before the 1950s hotel and tourist boom. It is made up of heath covered coastal hills that rise to 753m (2,470ft) and which are covered in beautifully scented wild flowers and herbs in spring and summer. The views of the coast and the glistening Mediterranean are wonderful and there are some 600 species of vascular plants—many of them endemic.

⊞ M5 ✉ 5km (3 miles) south of Dénia

SIERRA HELADA

These rugged mountains just to the north of Benidorm are named the 'ice mountains' not for their cold temperatures but for the way the moonlight glistens off their rocky boulders. They are riddled with caves, which were used by everyone from the Phoenicians pirates of the Spanish main and while villas cover most of the hills around Benidorm they have left this sierra largely untouched. Come in the early morning for wonderful walks and views and to beat the crowds.

⊞ K5 ✉ 2km (1.2 miles) north of Benidorm 🚌 From Benidorm

Whitewashed villas in Moraira (opposite); houses at the foot of the hills in Oliva (above)

Parc Natural de Montgó

VALL DE GALLINERA

This almond- and citrus-filled valley dotted with sleepy villages is one of the prettiest on the Costa Blanca. It is best seen from a tortuous road that winds from Pego near the coast to Planes. The area was settled by Christianized Moors until the 17th century, when they were expelled under the Inquisition—many of the villages and ruined dry-stone houses that line the valley were theirs.

➕ L3 ✉ 50km (31 miles) north of Benidorm 🍴 Restaurants and cafés

VALL DE GORGOS

It is easy to while away a couple of hours driving slowly through this pretty river valley which runs from the sierra to the coast near Jávea. It's filled with vineyards and citrus groves and dotted with handsome country houses whose huge arched porches were once used to hang and dry grapes to produce the raisins exported by the British from nearby Dénia and Jávea. The cane- and rattan-producing town of Gata—which straddles the main road—makes a good late lunch stop. Take your time to dine to ensure catching that beautiful golden light in the late afternoon.

➕ M5 ✉ 30km (18 miles) west of Benidorm 🍴 In Gata and dotted around the valley

VILLAJOYOSA

'The Jewelled Town' was a settlement in Roman times, a port for the Moors and a fortified fishing village protected against pirates after the Reconquest. Nowadays it is a popular international resort but it retains its Renaissance heart, centred on the Gothic church of Asunción and comprising narrow streets of pastel-paint houses. The town has a rowdy Moros y Cristianos festival in late July. For photos head to the El Casco Antiguo—the old town centre—in the late afternoon. It lies off the Plaza de la Generalitat and is made up of narrow Moorish streets lined with attractive houses. The most colourful are on Calle Mayor.

➕ K5 ✉ 10km (6 miles) south of Benidorm 🚉 🚌 From Benidorm

Fruit trees in the Vall de Gallinera

Vineyards in the Vall de Gorgos

A Night Walk Around Benidorm

This takes you through old Benidorm, along the seafront and through the bustling nightlife. It's best begun just before sunset.

DISTANCE: 2km (1.6 miles)   **ALLOW:** 2 hours with stops

START

WESTERN END OF BEACH
K5 🚌 None; take a taxi

END

EASTERN END OF BEACH
K5 🚌 None; take a taxi

① Begin at the western end of the esplanade on Playa Poniente—which until the early 1960s was a little fishing village—and walk up the stone steps into old Benidorm.

② Head to the end of the square and walk down the steps to the promontory that jutts out into the inky sea. There is no better place on the Costa Blanca to watch a sunset. The whole sweep of the resort lies to either side and as the sun sinks it burnishes the towering glass and concrete a deep gold.

③ Go inland and turn south to the Plaça de la Senyora, then walk down the steps to the left towards the jetty. Turn right along Paseig del Colon and right again onto Paseig de la Carretera. This was once the fishing village's main thoroughfare. On the left you'll see the entrance to the Mercado Municipal—with its stalls of fresh fish and Murcian vegetables.

⑥ After eating a late meal in a restaurant, finish your evening with a gentle stroll back to the hotel along the waterfront.

⑤ Turn left off the beach and inland along Calle Mallorca. This is the heart of British Benidorm and it's fun just to stroll around sampling the varied nightlife from the Belfast pubs and curry houses to the bingo and the variety shows.

④ Turn east and head to the coast and the beach and stroll along the beach esplanade that runs along Playa de Levante and drop into a beach bar for a cocktail.

A Drive to Guadalest and Cocentaina

The mountains immediately north of Benidorm are dotted with pretty Moorish villages and viewpoints offering enticing views.

DISTANCE: 110km (68 miles)   **ALLOW:** 8 hours, with stops

START

BENIDORM
✚ K5

END

BENIDORM

❶ Begin in Benidorm and take Route 70 (C3318) which leaves immediately north of the town at exit 65 on the E15 Alicante to Valencia motorway.

❷ After 7km (4 miles), turn right off the road following the signs for La Nucia. There are great views of the coast from here. Follow the road towards Callosa d'En. The road cuts through fruit plantations offering tantalizing views of the coast.

❸ Continue through the village of Callosa d'En to Guadalest (▷ 64–65) and take route CV715 east for 5km (3 miles). Follow signs for the Fuentes del Algar—a series of pretty waterfalls. Stop for a dip and a walk along the little trails that surround the River Algar.

❽ Return to Benidorm along Route 340 and the E15 motorway.

❼ Take Route 340 east to Cocentaina (▷ 70) and after visiting the Palau Comtal take tapas at Tracy Finch's Il Cavacici restaurant (▷ 81).

❻ Follow the road to Alcoy and spend the early afternoon exploring its Renaissance centre.

❺ Drive north from Guadalest on Route 70 to the whitewashed Moorish village of Confrides and cut through the Puerto de Ares pass.

❹ Return to Callosa d'En and, passing through the village, take route CV755 northwest to Guadalest. Visit the ruined castle and churches, taking an early lunch at the L'Hort restaurant (▷ 82).

Shopping

BARCELONA FOOTBALL WORLD

Benidorm is in the Comunidad de Valencia, which is closer culturally and linguistically to Catalonia than it is to Castillian Spain. So local allegiance in the great Real Madrid-Barca derbies is to the reds. You'll find all their paraphernalia here from shirts to posters, all with the correct 'official' badges and stamps essential to die-hard football fans.

➕ K5 ✉ Major Alameda between Martinez Alejos and Sol, Benidorm ☎ None 🕐 Mon–Sat 9.30–6.30

BENIDORM OUTDOOR MARKET

A mish-mash of goods and foodstuffs from Spanish cottons and lace, shoes, leather goods and clothing.

➕ K5 ✉ Calle Ibiza next to the Hotel Pueblo 🕐 Wed and Sun mornings.

CERAMICA LES SORTS

Beautiful practical pottery, objets d'art and ceramic ornaments made by artisans from all over Valencia and Murcia.

➕ L5 ✉ Edificio Kristal Mar 18D-18E, Moraira ☎ 965 74 57 37 🕐 Mon–Sat 9.30–6.30

EL CISNE FLEA MARKET

A mix of Portobello Road-style arts and crafts market and car boot sale with everything from junk shop goods, toys, LPs and CDs and second-hand clothing to arts and crafts.

➕ K5 ✉ At the junction of the Benidorm bypass and the N-332 towards Alfas del Pi 🕐 Sun 8–1 (also some Sat)

DELFOS

www.delfos-art.es
Paintings, sculptures, ceramics and objets d'art from a range of local and Spanish artists. Most are tasteful and expensive, and a few are genuine originals.

➕ K5 ✉ Calle Santa Faç 3, Benidorm ☎ 965 85 24 94 🕐 Mon–Sat 9.30–6.30

JOYERIA AMOR

Benidorm's most exclusive jeweller stocks a range of Spanish gold jewellery (which is 14 carat as opposed to 9 carat in the UK) alongside some stunning pieces from Italian designer brands.

➕ K5 ✉ Passeig Carretera 14, Benidorm ☎ 965 86 44 16 🕐 Mon–Sat 9.30–6.30

PACO LIMON

Hand, shoulder and beach bags in everything from beach-chic woven straw to soft as silk fine leather.

➕ K5 ✉ Plaça Major 41, Benidorm ☎ 965 85 34 60 🕐 Mon–Sat 9.30–6.30

PACO MARTINEZ

This is the shop to stop at if your suitcase splits or the wheels fall off your buggy-bag. There's a wide range of luggage here, large and small, plain and brightly coloured.

➕ K5 ✉ Avenida el Mediterráneo 24, Benidorm ☎ 965 85 25 18 🕐 Mon–Sat 9.30–6.30

PUR PEL

The Spanish love their shoes and many of them are made down the road in Elche. This street corner boutique offer a huge choice of everything from sandals to stilettos.

➕ K5 ✉ Calle Gambol between Martinez Alejos and Sol, Benidorm ☎ None 🕐 Mon–Sat 9.30–6.30

RITUAL

Hand- and factory-made Asian cotton and silk clothing and sarongs for men and women—perfect for the hot weather.

➕ M4 ✉ Marqués de Campo 26, Dénia ☎ 966 43 01 19 🕐 Mon–Sat 9.30–6.30

SANCT BERNHARD

Herbal remedies, essential oils, teas, cleansers and foodstuffs.

➕ L5 ✉ Avenida Gabriel Miró, Calpe ☎ 965 83 68 07 🕐 Mon–Sat 9.30–6.30

Entertainment and Activities

BAHAMAS

One of the beeriest and busiest of Benidorm's disco pubs. Young crowds and long happy hours.

➕ K5 ✉ Avenida Mallorca between Girona and Lepanto, Playa Levante, Benidorm ☎ 965 85 45 48

BAR DOMINO

www.bardomino.com

English-run bar and pub with a terrace overlooking the old town serving British beer and food and with free WiFi access.

➕ K5 ✉ Carrer Martinez Oriola 15, Benidorm ☎ 965 85 44 76 ⏱ Mon–Sat 11–5, 9–2, Sun 12–5

BENIDORM PALACE

www.benidormpalace.es

The town's grandest and most spectacular variety show. Comedians, magicians, live bands and an Iberian faux-Moulin Rouge dance show that's a gaudy riot of gyrating feather boas, high kicks and whoops. Dinner included; kids menu.

➕ K5 ✉ Avenida Severo Ochoa s/n, Benidorm ☎ 965 85 16 60 ⏱ Evenings

CABLE SKI

www.cableskibenidorm.com

This company offers water-skiing along and around Playa de Levante.

➕ K5 ✉ Racó de L'Oix, Benidorm ☎ 639 88 23 76

THE CELLAR

www.benidorm-spotlight.com/vincents-cellar

Clown and party fun for children with live shows and a bar for mums and dads.

➕ K5 ✉ Rincon de Loix, Benidorm ☎ No phone ⏱ From 5pm

CHAMPIONS

A busy pounding sports bar on the corner of the town's hen and stag party strip showing premiership and championship football and darts to a raucous, beer-drinking crowd.

➕ K5 ✉ Calle Mallorca s/n, Benidorm ☎ None ⏱ All day

FRATELLI FASHION BAR

A popular cocktail bar stopover at the heart of Playa Levante's party strip; offering tinkly music and a range of drinks including strong caipirinhas and icy mojitos.

ENTERTAINMENT

Benidorm offers a bewildering array of UK and Irish entertainment—much of it, aside from the clubs, rather old fashioned. Variety shows are played by circuit comedians, magicians, dance troupes and seventies and sixties tribute acts from the Bay City Rollers to the Rolling Stones. Most of the pubs show premiership football on football pitch-sized screens and British beers are widely available.

➕ K5 ✉ Calle Orts Llorca s/n, Benidorm ☎ 965 85 39 79

KARTING LA CALA

Spain's top go-kart track with eight-minute racing slots suitable for adults and children over 8.

➕ K5 ✉ Sierra Carretera Alicante-Valencia km 116, Benidorm ☎ 965 89 46 76 ⏱ Summer daily 10am–9pm; winter 10am–5pm

KM DISCO

www.kmdisco.com

One of a host of huge, pounding clubs on the Alicante road just north of Playa Levante. Music here is predominantly techno and the crowd busiest after 1am.

➕ K5 ✉ Careterra Alicante-Valencia km332, Benidorm 34 ☎ 965 86 35 23 ⏱ Easter–Oct 11pm–6am

KU LOUNGE

www.kubenidorm.es

Large terrace lounge bar on the esplanade with faux wicker tables and chairs shaded by towering date palms. A great spot for people-watching with a glass of sangria in hand. Doesn't attract stag and hen crowds.

➕ K5 ✉ Comunidad de Valencia, Benidorm ☎ None ⏱ Evenings

MARCO POLO EXPEDICIONES

www.marcopolo-exp.es

Trips up into the mountains behind Benidorm, including to

Guadalest in converted jeeps and coaches.

🏠 K5 ✉ Avenida Europa 5, Benidorm ☎ 965 86 33 99

MUNDOMAR
www.mundomar.es
A big marine park and sealife centre with old-fashioned dolphin shows, enclosures with sea lions and penguins, numerous tanks showcasing temperate and tropical fish species and a small zoo.

🏠 K5 ✉ Sierra Helada, Racó de L'Oix, Benidorm ☎ 965 86 01 00 🕐 Daily 10–6

PENÉLOPE
www.penelope.eu.com
Penélope Beach's dance club lies on the main club strip just opposite KM. The crowd here is similar if a little more Spanish and the music hip hop, techno and general Ibiza club. Big name DJs play in season.

🏠 K5 ✉ Carretera Alicante-Valencia km120, Benidorm ☎ 610 23 87 97 🕐 Easter–Oct 11pm–6am

PENÉLOPE BEACH
www.penelope.eu.com
Many Benidorm nights begin at this popular beachfront club. It gets lively after 11pm when DJs spin the turntables and professional dancers perform for the crowd.

🏠 K5 ✉ Avenida de Alcoi 10, Benidorm ☎ 965 86 33 60 🕐 Evenings

QUADS-KAYAKS
www.funquads.com
Quad bike and kayak adventures along the coast and in the mountains throughout the northern Costa Blanca.

🏠 M4 ✉ Consolát del Mar 8, Dénia ☎ 965 78 72 28 🕐 Daily 10–8.30

RANCHO SIERRA HELADA
Child-friendly gentle countryside pony and horse rides in the hills and coastal areas around Benidorm. Transport to the stables is included.

🏠 K5 ✉ Sierra Helada, Benidorm ☎ 678 98 31 19

SCUBA DIVING BENIDORM
www.scubadivingbenidorm. com
The Mediterranean has been almost fished out but there are some beautiful rock formations near Benidorm. The dive shop offers dives and PADI-certificated courses.

🏠 K5 ✉ Avenida Otto de

Habsburgo 10, Benidorm, ☎ 655 11 85 09 🕐 Daily

STARDUST
www.stardustbenidorm.com
An older crowd gathers here and in the club's myriad imitators throughout the town for old fashioned and very British variety and cabaret entertainment with live music, comedians and 'Spain's only Bay City Rollers tribute band'.

🏠 K5 ✉ Avenida Almería 1, Benidorm ☎ 965 85 38 44 🕐 Evenings

TERRA MÍTICA
www.terramiticapark.com
One of Spain's largest and most imaginative theme parks with a range of rides and roller-coasters themed in sections devoted to the Iberian, Egyptian, Roman and Greek civilizations.

🏠 K6 ✉ Careterra Benidorm-Finestrat, Benidorm ☎ 902 02 02 20 🕐 Summer daily 10–10 (some rides may close earlier)

VIVA
www.vivabarbenidorm.com
Lively gay bar in the heart of the old town playing pop, house and light club sounds and a long bar serving cocktails, international beers and snack food.

🏠 K5 ✉ Calle Alicante, Old Town, Benidorm ☎ 652 32 66 50 🕐 Daily 9pm–2.30am

NIGHTLIFE
Benidorm's beery bars and booming dance clubs are among the busiest and best appointed in Southern Spain. If you prefer to search out a local night out head for Alicante, Murcia or even Elche or Alcoy—in the latter you'll be pretty much the only foreigner in the establishment.

Restaurants

PRICES

Prices are approximate, based on a 3-course meal for one person.

€€€	over €40
€€	€20–€40
€	under €20

LA AGELMA (€€€)

www.mont-sant.com
The city's plushest restaurant is situated in this rustic chic hotel set in pretty gardens on the castle hill. The superlative cooking is traditional Valencian with a modern twist and the wine list is excellent. There are special children's and vegetarian menus.

➕ L2 ✉ Hotel Mont Sant, Subida al Castillo s/n, Jativa ☎ 962 27 50 81 ◷ Lunch and dinner

L'ALBUFERA/CASA PACO NADAL (€)

Tables are always busy with British and Spanish diners tucking into Spanish and international standards, grilled meat and fish and a wide variety of tapas.

➕ K5 ✉ Calle Girona 3, Benidorm ☎ 965 86 56 61 ◷ Lunch and dinner

CASA PATRICIO (€€)

Traditional Valencian rabbit and almond stews and other game dishes are served in this cosy family-run restaurant in the heart of the sierra, ten minutes drive from Guadalest.

➕ K4 ✉ Calle Arriba 37, Benidorm ☎ 965 88 53 10 ☎ Closed Mon

IL CAVACICI (€)

Good value dishes of the day, sandwiches and award-winning tapas—try the goat's cheese with pineapple curry sauce and a lively local bar crowd at night. English and Spanish-run.

➕ K3 ✉ Calle Comte de Cocentaina 9, Cocentaina ☎ 966 33 36 86 ◷ Mon–Tue, Thu, Sat 9am–midnight, Fri 5pm–midnight

EVEREST TANDOORI (€)

There's a huge eat-in and takeaway menu at this Indian restaurant a block from the beach and excellent value six-course lunch and dinner

specials for the very hungry. Children's menus also available.

➕ L5 ✉ Calle Joan de Garay, Calpe ☎ 965 83 90 45 ◷ Lunch and dinner. Stays open until after midnight in summer

HIMALAYA (€)

This Nepalese-run curry house is immensely popular with homesick Brits and offers a huge menu of standards from baltis to masalas to eat-in or take-away.

➕ K5 ✉ Calle Sant Pere 36, Altea ☎ 966 88 51 33 ◷ Lunch and dinner

L'HORT (€)

The food and furnishings are simple but the location the best in town—right next to the castle and with sweeping views of the valley from the terrace. For something uniquely Valencian try *mintxo*—a maize and vegetable pastry.

➕ K4 ✉ Calle La Virgen 1, Guadalest ☎ 965 88 52 69 ◷ Daily 10am–6pm

INTERNACIONAL (€€)

The terrace tables here come with a sweeping view of the beach and the extensive international and Spanish menu includes some of the best paellas in Benidorm.

➕ K5 ✉ Edificio Aguamarina, Playa de Levante, Benidorm ☎ 965 83 60 03 ◷ Lunch and dinner. Closed Jan, Feb

EL MOLINO (€)

The simple seafood served in this rustic chic tapas bar and restaurant is prepared with the freshest ingredients making it very popular with Spanish in the know. The bodega has the best Spanish wine list in the city.

🕂 K5 ✉ Avenida Comunidad Valenciana 123, Benidorm ☎ 965 85 71 81 🕐 Lunch and dinner

LA PALMERA (€€)

Traditional Valencian cooking including hearty rice and seafood dishes are served here, on an airy little terrace and to predominantly Spanish diners.

🕂 K5 ✉ Avenida Severo Ochoa 48, Benidorm ☎ 965 85 32 82 🕐 Daily lunch and dinner. Closed mid-Jan to mid-Feb

EL PI DEL SENYORET (€€)

www.elpidelsenyoret.es
A romantic little restaurant set in a garden shaded by olive trees just outside Altea town. The cooking is traditional Spanish and light Mediterranean and there's a little cocktail area for pre- or post-dinner relaxation.

🕂 K5 ✉ Partida Les Quintanes 7, Altea ☎ 966 88 55 44 🕐 Dinner only

EL POBLET (€€)

www.elpoblet.com
Great local rice dishes —especially the bursting-with-flavour prawns—and a breezy terrace view.

🕂 M4 ✉ Carretera Las Marinas km2, Dénia ☎ 965 78 54 79 🕐 Closed Sun, Mon and Feb–Mar

EL PULPO PIRATA (€)

Tucked away in the little fishing village at the heart of Benidorm is this refuge of local Spanish who come to eat the excellent choice of tapas and simple seafood on the shady al fresco terrace.

🕂 K5 ✉ Calle Tomás Ortuño 59, Benidorm ☎ 966 80 32 19 🕐 Lunch and dinner

TIFFANY'S (€€€)

www.restaurante-tiffanys.de
One of Benidorm's more sophisticated dining rooms with a wide selection of Mediterranean dishes, excellent seafood and a respectable wine list.

🕂 K5 ✉ Avenida del Mediterráneo 51, Edificio Coblanca 3, Benidorm ☎ 965 85 44 68 🕐 Dinner. Closed Mon, Jan and Feb

EATING BRITISH

Benidorm is packed with places serving British and Irish food, much of it of dubious quality. Pubs and cafés offer the great British or Irish breakfast, sausages, egg and chips and there are numerous curry houses and fish and chip takeaways. British haute cuisine has yet to make it to the Costa Blanca.

TUTTI FRUTTI PIZZERIA (€)

www.tuttifruttialtea.com
Pizza and pasta served in a brightly coloured children-friendly restaurant with special kid's menus, on the waterfront.

🕂 K5 ✉ Calle San Pere, Altea ☎ 966 88 10 40 🕐 Lunch and Dinner

VIVA ESPAÑA (€€€)

www.viva-espana.net
A big tourist restaurant with one of the largest flamenco dance shows on the coast at weekends in July and August, and a menu of Spanish standards, paellas and grilled meat and fish served all week.

🕂 M4 ✉ Carretera Valencia-Alicante km 216, Salida 61, Oliva, Dénia ☎ 962 85 19 31 🕐 Dinner only

LOS ZAPATOS (€€)

This cosy, intimate dining room just a block from the beach serves an interesting eclectic menu with Spanish-Asian fusion options like chicken breast in Thai curry sauce and traditional options like oxtail al Monastrell.

🕂 L5 ✉ Calle Santa Marta, Calpe ☎ 965 83 15 07 🕐 Summer dinner only; winter Thu–Mon 1–3.30pm and 7–11pm. Closed 2 weeks in Jan

Murcia is a provincial city with a magnificent cathedral. It's in dry countryside with irrigated agriculture and golf courses broken by stretches of forest-covered hills. The *comunidad* is less touristy than Alicante or Benidorm and its mountain villages and beaches are far quieter.

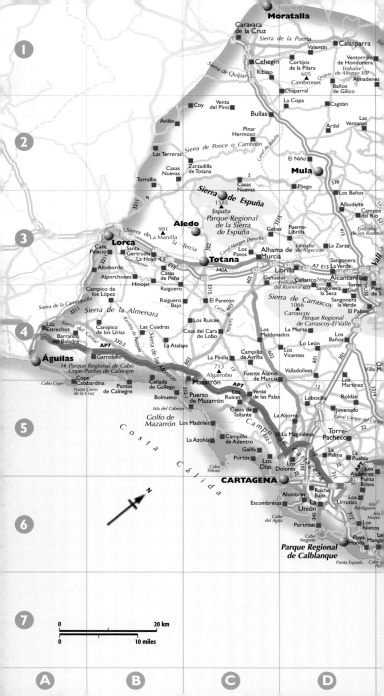

Calblanque

HIGHLIGHTS

- Beaches
- Dunes
- Coastal walks
- Wild flowers in spring
- Bird life
- Loggerhead turtle nesting beaches

TIP

- Arrive early in the morning to catch the golden early light and the fewest people.

For unspoiled beaches head for this stretch of rocky bays and sandy coves south of the busy condominiums of the Mar Menor salt lake. There are none less spoiled or visited on the Costa Blanca.

Natural park It's thanks to the vigilance and fighting spirit of local Murcians that there is any undeveloped coastline on the Costa Blanca. They fought hard in the 1980s to ensure that Calblanque be set aside as a protected Natural Park. Access is down a rocky track off the main coastal highway to Aguilas. A little car park leads to coastal footpaths and boardwalks that cut across a series of shale dunes thick with fossils to the sandy beaches. The best is Playa Larga—with excellent swimming in clear water and decent snorkelling off the rocky headlands at the far end.

The beaches at Calblanque (left); the rocky shoreline around Calblanque (right)

Viewpoints The coastal footpaths lead over gently sloping hills fronted by scrub-covered cliffs, which are covered in wild flowers in spring, to a number of coastal lookouts. The best of these is at Punta Negra where a lighthouse sits over strangely eroded rocks washed by the Mediterranean.

Wildlife Calblanque is rich in plant and animal life. Monk seals lay on the sand well into the 20th century but are sadly gone. However, some of the few surviving loggerhead turtle nesting beaches in developed Southern Spain remain and there is abundant bird life including spectacular raptors like the royal owl and rarer shore birds like black-winged stilt, avocets, greater flamingos and sand plovers (including the very rare greater sand plover). Mammals include abundant cape hares and stone martens.

THE BASICS

➕ D6
✉ 70km (43 miles) east of Murcia
☎ None
🕐 Tue–Sun 10–12, 2–7
🍴 None

Moratalla

Moratalla seen from its church (left); the castillo (right)

THE BASICS

www.moratalla-turismo.com

🔾 C1

🍴 Many small restaurants and a few hotels

♿ None

HIGHLIGHTS

● Castle
● Medieval and Moorish town centre
● Iglesia de la Asuncion
● Walking in the Sierra de los Alamos

TIP

● Book hotels well ahead for the running of the bulls festivals.

To really get beyond the tourist crowds head for this sleepy mountain village in the remote corner of Murcia. It's every bit as pretty and historic as Guadalest or Jativa but it receives a fraction of the visitors of either.

Historic town Moratalla is a Moorish huddle of ancient terracotta, baroque and Romanesque churches and Moorish battlements crowded into cobbled streets mountain-steep, bathed in history and barely as wide as a mule. Like many of the region's mountain towns it's built around a crumbling castle. Although lacking the wealth of Jativa or Orihuela, Moratalla also lacks the ugly modern hinterland that surrounds both; and it feels more medieval than either. Time seems to have stood still here since the Renaissance Reconquest when Moratalla was a lonely, dangerous Christian outpost lost in forbidding wild hills. Even the religious buildings attest to this. The tiny windows and bulky walls of the Renaissance Iglesia de la Asunción look as strong and defensive as a fort.

Attractions Moratalla's running of the bulls in July is famous throughout Murcia. And during Holy Week festival parades of *tamborista* drummers walk the streets dressed in hand-stitched pseudo-medieval robes. *Tamboradas* are characteristic only of Moratalla, Mula and a few other towns in Murcia. The surrounding Sierra de los Alamos mountains are dripping with little waterfalls. There's excellent walking and birding and fewer crowds than any other wild area in the region.

The old centre of Mula is dominated by its churches

Mula

Together with Moratalla in the remote north, Mula is the best-preserved of Murcia's medieval mountain villages. Its streets are whisper-quiet for most of the year but erupt in riotous festival celebrations in *Semana Santa* (Holy Week).

Walk the streets Mula's old centre is an enchanting conglomeration of narrow, higgledy-piggledy streets clinging to a steep hillside and topped by a massive castle. Begin a tour in the Glorieta Juan Carlos I gardens next to the Renaissance church of San Francisco. Across the way sits the Palácio de los Marquesas de Menahermosa, a modest, late baroque palace decorated with azure floral patterns whose Museo de Arte Ibérico El Cigarralejo museum preserves one of the region's largest repositories of Iberian art. The Calle del Caño winds its way up the hill from the palace and eventually towards the castle. There are interesting townhouses and churches in the side streets. These include the 16th-century Renaissance churches of Santo Domingo and San Miguel and the more ornate 17th-century Iglesia de Carmen. The castle itself is a semi-ruin collapsing around a massive Moorish tower but the views out over the terracotta roofs, the river and the plains more than compensate for the climb.

Holy Week The best time to visit Mula is Holy Week when the town celebrates Easter with *tamborada* parades that are unique to Murcia and on this scale only in Moratalla. The streets rattle to thousands of *tambor* drums.

THE BASICS

www.aytomula.es
🔲 D2
✉ 32km (30 miles) west of Murcia
Museo de Arte Ibérico El Cigarralejo
www.museosdemurcia.com/cigarralejo/
✉ Calle Del Marqués 1
☎ 968 66 14 22
🕐 Mon–Fri 9–2, Sat 9.30–2
💶 Inexpensive

HIGHLIGHTS

● Winding alleys and crumbling mansions
● View from the castle
● Museo de Arte Ibérico El Cigarralejo
● Glorieta Juan Carlos I gardens

TIP

● If you can't make it to Semana Santa, Mula has another spectacular religious parade—the Romeria Del Niño Jesús de Balate parade, on 22 September.

MURCIA

★

TOP 25

HIGHLIGHTS

- Cathedral
- Casino
- Calle Trapería
- University
- Murcian tapas

TIP

- The cathedral is particularly impressive at night when it is beautifully illuminated.

Modern Murcia sprawls untidily along the banks of the Rio Segura, but hides a delightful Renaissance city at its heart, whose tiny streets are dominated by the baroque Catedral de Santa María.

History Although there have been settlements near modern Murcia for thousands of years, Murcia itself became a city under the Muslims after the fall of the Omayyad Caliphate of Córdoba in the 11th century. It expanded further after the battle of Sagrajas in 1086 when the Almoravid dynasty united the rival kingdoms of Islamic Spain. Ferdinand III of Castile conquered the city 1243.

Attractions From Moorish times the source of Murcia's wealth was agriculture, founded on the extensive *huerta* market gardens whose produce

Clockwise from left: Glorieta de España; a café in Trapería Street; the Puente Viejo; shopping on Trapería Street; another view of the Puente Viejo

remains the mainstay of Murcian regional cooking to this day. It reached the height of its prosperity in the 18th century under the Bourbons. Most of the city's finest buildings date from this period. They include the Iglesia Catedral de Santa María, one of the most lavish baroque buildings in Spain, and a string of handsome civic buildings dotted in and around the Plaza del Cardenal Belluga. These include the Palacio Episcopal and the buildings of the pedestrianized Calle Trapería, whose pavements are dotted with open-air café tables, where you can sample the tapas for which Murcia is famous. The city is also home to a beautiful baroque university and theatre (Teatro Romea), a selection of small art and archaeological museums and a remarkable faux-Moorish art nouveau casino by Pedro Cerdán Martínez, who was also responsible for Novelda's Casa Museo (▷ 37).

THE BASICS

www.murciaturistica.es

➕ E4

🍴 Many excellent restaurants and tapas bars

♿ Some

🚌 From Alicante

ℹ Plaza del Cardenal Belluga, tel 968 35 87 49; Mon–Sat 10–2, 4.30–8.30, Sun 10–2.
Calle Clara, Detrás del Teatro Romea, tel 968 22 06 59; Mon–Sat 10–2, 4.30–6.30

Murcia: Catedral de Santa María

HIGHLIGHTS

● View from Plaza del Cardenal Belluga
● The 16th-century bell tower
● Façade by Jaime Bort
● Capilla de los Vélez
● Capilla de Junterónes

TIP

● Come as early as possible in high season to avoid the coach party crowds.

Baroque buildings on the Costa Blanca come no grander than this. Santa María is one of the most impressive churches in Southern Spain.

The exterior What Santa María lacks in architectural unity it more than makes up for in grandeur and size. Its bizarre and richly ornamented neoclassical baroque façade encrusted with elaborate baroque tablets and gesticulating saints and aristocrats of varying proportions dwarfs the four- and five-floor mansions that crowd around it. Its massive, heavy Renaissance bell tower, which is the highest in Spain, stretches into the permanently blue sky like a giant minaret. Both sit somewhat at odds not only with each other but with the rest of the church (whose architectural styles range from late Romanesque to Renaissance). Yet somehow

From left: The exterior and a detail of the stonework; the interior

it all fits together magnificently. The odd conglomeration of styles reflects the church's past—building lasted from the 14th century to the late 18th.

Look inside The cathedral's interior is no less overpowering, an expanse of spartan Gothic offset with Renaissance, Churrigueresque and Mudejar carved ornamentation which reaches its most ornate in two exquisite chapels. At the far northern end of the church behind the Altar Mayor, the Capilla de los Vélez is a Gothic chapel rich with Mudejar carving whose fan vaulting meets to form a glorious, mandala-like cupola. At the other end of the nave, immediately to the south of the choir, is the Capilla de Junterónes. This is Renaissance in form but its decorative carving by Gil Rodríguez de Junterón (some of the finest in Spain) is almost baroque in its rich and exuberant detail.

THE BASICS

www.murciaciudad.com/catedral.htm

🔳 j3

✉ Plaza del Cardenal Belluga

☎ 968 22 13 71

🕐 Daily 10–1, 5–7

🍴 Many small restaurants and the excellent Mont Sant on castle hill (▷ 111)

♿ Good

🎟 Free; sacred art museum: moderate

Sierra de Espuña

Castillo de los Velos, Mula (left); forests of Sierra d'Espuna (right); monastery the hills (opposite)

THE BASICS

www.sierraespuna.com

C3

25km (15.5 miles) south of Alicante

Restaurants in Mula, Alhama and Aledo

None

Tours and over-night stays with Louisa Livingstone (www.nestwalks.info) or Espuña Adventure (www.espuna-adventure.com)

HIGHLIGHTS

● The mountain views
● The royal eagle
● Iberian wild cat
● Camping overnight
● Climbing the Pico de Espuña

TIP

● Even when it's warm on the coast it can get chilly in the Sierra—bring a light jumper and a raincoat.

These rugged mountains southwest of Murcia are one of the few remaining pockets of unspoiled wild on the Costa Blanca. The sleepy Renaissance village of Mula is the perfect base for visiting them

Flora and fauna But for a proliferating florescence of brilliant green golf courses, much of Murcia is dry. So it's hard to imagine that in the late 19th century many villages in southwest Murcia were frequently destroyed by flash floods, which would rush down from the deforested slopes of the Sierra de Espuña. As a result, the Murcian government embarked on one of the world's first major re-forestation projects; carpeting the Sierra's denuded slopes with cedar, cypress, juniper and pine. Since then biodiversity has bloomed—vascular plant species numbers have reached over 1,000. There are plenty of wild animals too, with eight species of amphibians, 17 reptiles and 38 mammals including an endemic sub-species of red squirrel and wild cat, ibex, barbary sheep and herds of boar. Most spectacular are the 123 species of birds, including three species of eagle: the short-toed eagle, Bonelli's eagle and the endangered royal eagle.

Visit You can get an idea of the sierra on a drive, with stops for strolls to waterfalls and to picnic. But to get into the wilder areas or climb the Sierra's highest peak, the 1,579m (5,179ft) Pico de Espuña, you'll need at least a day. Camping overnight is possible and a handful of companies organize nature walks.

More to See

ÁGUILAS

www.aguilas.es

For a purely Spanish beach resort well-off the northern European package holiday circuit head south to this town on the edge of the Golfo de Mazarrón. The town has an interesting old fishing port centre watched over by a small castle and two long, broad beaches.

➕ A4 ✉ 80km (49 miles) south of Murcia 🍴 Restaurants and cafés 🚌 From Murcia

ALEDO

There are wonderful views over the coast from this little Moorish town. Just outside town is the little-visited Ermita de Santa Eulalia church with a richly carved Mudejar ceiling which depicts the persecution and murder of the saint by Roman centurions. On 7 December the Ermita receives thousands of pilgrims. The town, in the foothills of the Sierra de Espuña, is a good base for exploring the park.

➕ C3 ✉ 43km (27 miles) southwest of Murcia 🍴 Some restaurants 🚌 From Murcia

CARTAGENA

www.cartagena.es

Murcia's second city is a busy coastal town that takes its name from Hannibal's capital, Carthage—which is in Africa—and lends it to one of the most famous and romantic colonial ports in the Americas. Modern, Iberian Cartagena lacks the romance of the former, and the crumbling tropical beauty of the latter. But it looks over an impressive natural harbour and is replete with handsome buildings and churches (including one of Spain's oldest—Santa Maria). The city's Museo Arqueológico Municipal and the Museo Nacional de Arqueológica Marítima both contain important Roman collections and there is a lively festival in Holy Week when thousands of visitors from Spain come to see the lengthy processions, floats and firework displays.

➕ D6 ✉ 53km (33 miles) south of Murcia 🍴 Restaurants and cafés 🚌 From Murcia 🚌 From Murcia

Museo Arqueológico Municipal

✉ Calles Ramon y Cajal 45

The beach at San Juan de los Terreros near Águilas

Spa buildings, partially obscured by trees, at Fortuna

☎ 968 53 90 27 🕐 Tue–Fri 10–2, 5–8, Sat, Sun 11–2 ✋ Free

Museo Nacional de Arqueológica Marítima
✉ Paseo Alfonso XII 22 ☎ 968 12 11 66 🕐 Tue–Sat 10–7.30, Sun 10–3 ✋ Free

FORTUNA: HOT SPRINGS

The Romans and Arabs alike celebrated the purity and medicinal properties of these hot springs just outside the dull, industrial town of Fortuna. The Spanish built a spa here in the 19th century which still stands and gives the springs an old-fashioned feel, with marble baths, a steaming open-air pool and a range of hearty massages.
➕ F3 ✉ 22km (13.5 miles) north of Murcia ☎ 968 68 50 11 🕐 Daily 8–1, pool 10–9 ✋ Moderate 🚌 From Murcia

JUMILLA

The vineyards in this agricultural castle town in far northern Murcia are some of Europe's oldest. They were first planted by the Romans and are some of the few in Europe not to have been decimated by the phylloxera outbreak that devastated France and northern Spain in the 19th century. While far from Spain's best, the reds are intense and have a very high alcohol content.
➕ F1 ✉ 55km (34 miles) north of Murcia 🍴 Restaurants 🚌 From Murcia

LORCA
www.lorca.es

This elegant town huddled around a 13th-century fortress preserves some of the finest baroque buildings in Murcia. Highlights include the splendid Ex-Colegiata de San Patricio, a Renaissance church with a beautiful baroque interior. The church was built in celebration of a series of military victories against the Moors on the feast day of San Patricio in 1452—although the interior is mostly 18th century. Lorca also has a series of exquisite civil buildings, with streets of handsome town houses and a beautiful town hall (*ayuntamiento*). Some of the finest buildings are gathered around the Ex-colegiata on the Plaza España. An imposing, ruined 13th-century castle watches over the

★

Looking down across Cartegena

San Mateo church in Lorca

city. Like many other cities in Murcia, Lorca hosts spectacular Holy Week celebrations. It also hosts an annual rock festival usually in the summer.

➕ B3 ✉ 55km (34 miles) southwest of Murcia 🍴 Restaurants 🚌 From Murcia

MAR MENOR

www.marmenor.es

The Mar Menor (smaller sea) is a vast and shallow salt lagoon that stretches for some 15km (7 miles) between San Pedro del Pintar in the northeast and Cabo de Palos in the southwest. Its Mediterranean channel, a 24km-long (15-mile) strip of sand barely a kilometre (half a mile) wide was an important breeding site for hundreds of rare birds until the 1960s. Today it is backed by a phalanx of hotels and condominiums geared-up for the influx of (mostly Spanish) summer visitors. The lagoon's flat, shallow waters offer excellent windsurfing, sailing and water-skiing.

➕ E6 ✉ 55km (34 miles) southwest of Murcia 🍴 Restaurants 🚌 From Murcia 🚌 From Murcia

TOTANA

www.totana.net

This unprepossessing town, famous throughout Spain for its pottery, lies a short drive from Murcia along the motorway to the southwest. There are still some 20 family-run businesses here, many of them utilizing Arab-style kilns with a perforated and heated floor on which the baking urns, plates and pots are fired. The bargains are in the town centre, not in the tourist shops on the main road.

➕ C3 ✉ 35km (22 miles) southwest of Murcia 🍴 Restaurants 🚌 From Murcia

VALL DE SEGURA

Many of Murcia's fruits and vegetables come from this green valley filled with with citrus groves, almonds, rice fields and an ever-expanding proliferation of low, ugly and sadly disposable polythene greenhouses. It has been planted since Roman times and offers an alternative to the drive through the Gallinera valley in Benidorm (▷ 74).

➕ E3 ✉ 30km (18.5 miles) northwest of Murcia 🚌 From Murcia

The view across the Segura Valley

The stone lighthouse in Labo de los Palos, Mar Menor

Murcia's Old Centre

The filigree of streets that make up old Murcia crowd around the city's lavish and monumental cathedral and are filled with delightful little tapas bars and traditional restaurants.

DISTANCE: 2.5km (1.6 miles)   **ALLOW:** 2 hours, with stops

START

PLAZA SANTO DOMINGO
➕ j2 🚌 From town centre or rail station

❶ Begin at the Plaza Santo Domingo, a huge square filled with flower stalls and lined with a proliferation of pavement bars, cafés and tapas houses.

❷ Walk from here past the smart boutiques that line Calle Trapería to the Casino (▷ 103). This delightful fantasy palace with its mock-Mudejar doors and lavish art nouveau flourishes was built by Pedro Cerdán Martínez who was also responsible for Novelda's beautiful Casa Museo Moderna.

❸ Continue from here along Calle Escultor Salzillo to the city's magnificent cathedral (▷ 92–93) which has the tallest church tower in Spain and a lavish, sculpture adorned façade.

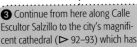

END

PLAZA SANTO DOMINGO

❻ Take the fifth turning on the right onto Calle Platería and from here, the third street on the left. This brings you back to the Plaza de Santo Domingo via the pretty in pink 19th-century Teatro Romea.

❺ Turn right at the Glorieta España onto the Via Escultor Salzillo. This is the heart of modern Murcia and is the city's most fashionable shopping district. Spend some time browsing in the boutiques as you wander along the street.

❹ After marvelling at the church's ornate baroque interior, walk to the modest Renaissance bishop's palace opposite the cathedral and from there towards the river.

MURCIA

WALK

99

Through the Sierra

The Sierra de Espuña offers views and clear mountain air and on this drive you can enjoy both and some pretty mountain villages.

DISTANCE: 100km (62 miles)   **ALLOW:** 8 hours, with stops

START

MURCIA
➕ E4

END

MURCIA

❶ Leave Murcia early on the E15 motorway and take the turn-off after around 45km (28 miles) for the MU502 and the mountain town of Aledo.

❽ Spend the afternoon exploring Mula and take the C451 back to the E15 motorway arriving back in Murcia in the early evening.

❷ After a *café con leche* and breakfast in a local bar and a swift visit to the Ermita de Santa Eulalia church (▷ 96) follow the signs to the Sierra de Espuña Regional Park, which lies north off the road just outside town.

❼ Continue on the C3315 to Mula (▷ 89) and take a late lunch at the Venta La Magdalena restaurant (▷ 105).

❸ Grab a map from the information booth at the park entrance and drive up the twisting road into the hills.

❻ Exit the park via the little villages of El Berro and Gebas, the latter of which has great views out over the Sierra. Stop at the village of Pliego to admire the ruined castle tower. This was an important town on the transhumance routes that once traversed Europe and which were used by migratory shepherds and their flocks.

❹ Turn left at the signpost for the *pozos de nieve* (named after the ice wells that once functioned here).

❺ Park in the little car park and after admiring the beautiful views, take a short hike into the park along one of the marked trails.

DRIVE

MURCIA

Shopping

ALFARERÍA BELLÓN

One of the best-known of Totana's various ceramicists, making contemporary pottery using the town's traditional techniques.

➕ C3 ✉ Paseo Ollería 19, Totana ☎ 968 42 48 01

ARTESANÍA ABELLÁN

A wide range of mostly religious arts and crafts including beautiful, handmade crib figures.

➕ Off map at l1 ✉ Calle Mayor 16, Barrio del Progreso, Murcia ☎ 968 25 28 06

BERSHKA

www.bershka.com

One of the better labels for young, vibrant Spanish street fashion with a range of clothes to suit the city or the beach.

➕ j2 ✉ Gran Vía Escultor Francisco Salzillo 21, Murcia ☎ 968 28 13 50

CALLE JABONERIAS

This narrow alley in the city centre is crammed with lots of quirky little boutiques and international designer names. Prices are high but so is quality and there are often bargains to be found, especially for shoes and Spanish fashion labels.

➕ j2 ✉ Centro, Murcia ☎ No phone

CENTRO REGIONAL DE ARTESANÍA

An exhibition space and shop devoted to showcasing traditional Murcian craftware from pottery to knitware and weavework.

➕ j2 ✉ Calle Francisco Rabal 8, Murcia ☎ 968 35 75 37

EL CORTE INGLES

www.elcorteingles.es.

Murcia boasts two branches of Spain's largest department store chain, where you can stock up on everything from Spanish music to wine, food, fashion and electronic items.

➕ j2 ✉ Avenida de la Libertad s/n and Gran Vía Escultor Salzillo, Murcia ☎ 968 29 80 50

FONDA NEGRA

One of the best places in the city to buy regional wines and foodstuffs.

➕ j2 ✉ González Adalid 1, Murcia ☎ 968 21 15 63

JERONIMO DE RODA MARKET

A large bric-à-brac and bargain clothes market with a vast array of stalls and makeshift shops selling everything from CDs to jewellery, clothing and foodstuffs.

➕ h2 ✉ Calle Jeronimo de Roda, just behind El Corte Inglés, Murcia

MERCADO DE LAS VERONICAS

A large covered food market stocking the best and freshest fruit, vegetables and other groceries.

➕ h2 ✉ Plano de San Francisco, Murcia

PASTELERIA CARLOS

A huge range of delicious, sweet cakes and pastries.

➕ j3 ✉ Jaime el Conquistador 7, Murcia ☎ 968 23 30 20

EL POVEO

One of the largest and best-known of Totana's ceramic producers offering a variety of ornamental and practical pots, plates and decorative items for the home.

➕ C3 ✉ Calle Rambla s/n, Totana ☎ 968 42 19 52

YELMO ANTIGÜEDADES

www.yelmoantiguedades.com

A wonderful range of (expensive) antiques from all over Iberia in one of the best showrooms in the region.

➕ D6 ✉ Calle Sagasta 34, Cartagena ☎ 968 52 54 13

SPANISH MUSIC

Music is one of the best Spanish buys on the Costa Blanca and can be listened to prior to buying at the larger department stores like El Corte Inglés. For classic flamenco, check out Paço de Lucia and El Camarón de la Isla and for more modern flamenco pop, Ketama and Niña Pastori. Other interesting Spanish artists include Manu Chao, Radio Tarifa and Israeli flamenco singer Yasmin Levy.

Entertainment and Activities

CAFÉ DEL ARTE
A cool bar and club with big porthole windows, cocktails and a 20-something crowd. Kicks off around 11pm and has dance music from local DJs at weekends.
➕ D6 ✉ Avenida del Mediterraneo, Cartegena ☎ None ⏰ Nightly

CASINO MURCIA
The city's gorgeous art nouveau treasure is no mere monument, it is also one of Spain's most famous casinos.
➕ j3 ✉ Calle Apostoles 34, Murcia ☎ 968 50 10 10 ⏰ Daily 10–2, 5–11

DNC
The city's premier nightclub is packed with students and plays a mix of Spanish and European club music and club standards in English. Begins to fill in the small hours at the weekends and pumps away until after dawn.
➕ k2 ✉ Calle Puerta Nueva, Edificio Centrofama, Universidad, Murcia ☎ 676 21 90 13 ⏰ Check locally

GARAJE DE TIA MARIA
One of the city's staunch rock venues with some great small international and local live acts on weekends and a mix of Spanish and international rock and pop on the speakers throughout the week.
➕ j3 ✉ Calle Miguel de Cervantes 43, Murcia ☎ None ⏰ Check locally

KALLEJÓN
One of the largest dance clubs in Murcia with two heaving floors of Spanish techno and house and a range of international standards. Occasional big-name Spanish DJs.
➕ l1 ✉ Calle Ceuti s/n, Pol. Industrial Atalayas, Afueras, Murcia ☎ None ⏰ Check locally

EL MENTIDERO
A popular bar de copas—or drinking hole for young Murcians with occasional DJs and live bands at weekends and an eclectic weekend clientele.
➕ k2 ✉ Calle Saavedra Fajardo 3, Universidad, Murcia ☎ 968 22 35 33 ⏰ Daily 3pm–3am

---

GOLF
The Costa Blanca is replete with golf courses, many designed by stars like Jack Niklaus or Seve Ballesteros. It is easy to find a game. Golf courses in the region—especially Murcia—have come under heavy criticism from environmentalists and local farmers for their flouting of EU green guidelines and heavy use of water in a severely drought-stricken area. Murcia has been rocked by a series of corruption scandals involving local politicians and the real estate construction industry.

MUNDAKA
www.mundakaclub.com
The most popular dance club in Murcia with three floors of dance, lounge and chill-out areas. International music.
➕ j2 ✉ Carretera Santa Catalina 26, Murcia ☎ None ⏰ Lounge Mon–Fri 8pm–3am, Sat–Sun 3–3; club Fri–Sat from 2am, Sun from 6pm

ROYAL PALACE
A vast Spanish and Hispanic-American dance club in a multi-level venue with space for 2,000 people. The crowd is predominantly 30-something.
➕ j2 ✉ Carretera Santa Catalina 17, Afueras, Murcia ☎ 968 26 79 83 ⏰ Check locally

TEATRO ROMEA
www.teatroromea.org
The city's principal drama and live classical music and dance venue. Also plays host to world music stars and jazz.
➕ j2 ✉ Plaza Julián Romea 7, Murcia ☎ 968 35 53 90 or 968 35 51 70 (box office) ⏰ Check locally

UNDERGROUND
www.undergroundnoche.com
A club and live music venue with a variety of live acts and divergent entertainment all week, from DJs and live bands to variety and comedians.
➕ D6 ✉ Calle Condesa Calderón, Cartagena ☎ 968 12 61 05 ⏰ Check locally

Restaurants

ACUÁRIO (€€)

A traditional Murcia restaurant a few hundred yards from the cathedral famous for its *merluza* (hake) and *berinjela con champiñón y jamón* (aubergine with ham and mushroom).

🔒 j2 ✉ Plaza Puxmarina 3, Murcia ☎ 968 21 99 55 🕐 Mon–Sat lunch and dinner

LA BUENA TAPA (€€)

This restaurant just north of the centre in the Cabezo de Torres neighbourhood is the place to come for a paella—traditionally served at midday and the weekend.

🔒 Off map at h1 ✉ Calle Jaime 1, 7, Murcia ☎ 968 93 12 40 🕐 Lunch and dinner

LAS CADENAS (€€)

A formal dining room in the shadow of the cathedral serving regional specialities like *alcachofas con almeias* (artichoke with almonds), *lubina* (sea bass) and *pastel de cebolla* (onion tart). Excellent wine list.

🔒 j3 ✉ Calle Apóstoles 10, Murcia ☎ 968 22 09 24 🕐 Mon–Sat 1.30–4.30pm, 8.30–11pm

CASA CÁNDIDO (€€)

A very traditional Murcian restaurant housed in a 16th-century building, which offers local dishes that include delicious stuffed baby squid and roast leg of kid.

🔒 B3 ✉ Calle Santo Domingo 13, Lorca ☎ 968 46 69 07 🕐 Lunch and dinner

EL CHURRA (€–€€)

A range of small but spruce rooms all with internet and an excellent little restaurant and tapas bar. There is parking for those brave enough to brave the labyrinthine streets of central Murcia—with an extra charge.

🔒 j1 ✉ Avenida Marqués del los Vélez 12, Murcia ☎ 968 23 84 00 🕐 Lunch and dinner

EL CIGARRALEJO (€€€)

One of the better seafood restaurants in inland

Murcia renowned for its ultra-fresh fish and excellent prawns and paellas, which should be requested in advance.

🔒 D2 ✉ Carretera de Pliego s/n, Mula ☎ 968 662 105 🕐 Lunch and dinner

DELDADO (€)

Some of the best ice cream in southern Spain is handmade on the premises in this little café next to the cathedral.

🔒 j3 ✉ Bajo la Torre de la Catedral, Murcia ☎ 656 41 90 76 🕐 Daily 3–11pm

LOS HABANEROS (€–€€)

This lively hotel restaurant serves some of the city's best fish, with exquisite *solomillo en salsa con almejas* (fish steak in clam sauce) and *rape Habaneros* (Havana monkfish).

🔒 D6 ✉ Calle San Diego 60, Cartagena ☎ 968 50 52 50 🕐 Lunch and dinner

HISPANO (€€)

Another regional and traditionally Spanish restaurant renowned for its outstanding vegetable dishes, meat and fish and with an excellent wine list.

🔒 j2 ✉ Calle Arquitecto Cerdán 7, Murcia ☎ 968 21 61 52 🕐 Closed Sun dinner and Aug

LA HUERTANICA (€€)

A favourite for its traditional Murcian cooking. Alongside the main dishes there are more

than 60 varieties of tapas, a decent wine list and cold draught beer.

🔒 J2 ✉ Calle Infantes 3, Murcia ☎ 968 21 76 68
🕐 Lunch and dinner

MARENOSTRUM (€€€)
www.marenostrum.es
The city's most famous seafood restaurant is housed in a modern building from where there are superb views out over the port. The paellas are excellent.

🔒 D6 ✉ Paseo de Alfonso XII, Puerto Deportivo, Cartagena ☎ 968 52 21 31 or 968 52 92 15 🕐 Lunch and dinner

EL OLIVAR (€€€)
This apparently rustic local restaurant serves some of the finest food in Spain. Firo Vázquez de Parga's prize-winning fare is simple but beautifully prepared using the very best ingredients. It's worth coming here just for the home-grown and pressed olive oil. Reserve a table on the pretty terrace and order the *conejo al ajo cabañil* (rabbit in garlic) or the *lubina* (sea bass) for a special dining experience.

🔒 C1 ✉ Carretera de Caravaca 50, Moratalla ☎ 968 72 40 54 🕐 Closed Mon and Tue

RAIMUNDO (€€)
Murcia's most famous regional restaurant is in one of its most beautiful buildings—the Casino.

Try the *dorada al estilo pescador* (fisherman's gilthead bream) accompanied by *verduras de la huerta* (garden vegetables).

🔒 J3 ✉ Calle Trapería 22, Murcia ☎ 968 22 06 58
🕐 Lunch and dinner. Closed Sun pm, Mon and Aug

RESTAURANTE EL PARADOR (€€)
www.paradordelmarmenor.com
One of the region's finest and most beautiful restaurants is set in a converted mansion house with shady palm-filled gardens overlooking the beach. Cooking is Mediterranean.

🔒 E6 ✉ El Vivero, Playa de los Alemanes, La Manga ☎ 968 56 38 73 🕐 Lunch and dinner. Closed Tue

VENTA LA MAGDALENA (€)
Come here for excellent and unpretentious provincial Murcian cooking.

🔒 D2 ✉ Carretera Caravaca km 21, Mula ☎ 968 66 05 68
🕐 Lunch and dinner

THE HUERTA
The fertile flatlands, or *huerta*, around Murcia are one of the largest exporters of vegetables in Europe—most of it shipped out from under the acres of plastic on refrigerated lorries. The best produce remains in Spain—around Murcia and is a key ingredient in many of the regional tapas dishes.

LA VELETA (€€€)
www.restaurantelaveleta.es
This modernist restaurant and tapas bar serves wonderful fish and the city's famous *gambas rojas* (red prawns).

🔒 A4 ✉ Calle de Blas Rosique 6, Águilas ☎ 968 41 17 98 🕐 Lunch and dinner

VIRGEN DEL MAR (€€–€€€)
There are wonderful sea views from this luxuriously decorated terrace restaurant. The kitchen is famous for its typically Murcian *albóndigas de merluza* (hake balls) and its *croquetas de gambas* (prawn croquettes).

🔒 C4 ✉ Paseo Marítimo s/n, Mazarrón ☎ 968 59 50 57 🕐 Lunch and dinner. Closed Nov

LOS ZAGALES (€)
Murcia's best tapas are served at this unpretentious little restaurant a stone's throw from the cathedral. It's decorated with pictures of local *toreros* (bullfighters) and football stars and the menu is enormous. Favourites include delicious *empanadillas rellenas de ensaladilla y pimiento*—little pasties filled with salad and pepper, mini-sandwiches or *bocadillitos* and a choice of rich Spanish cheeses.

🔒 E4 ✉ Calle Polo de Medina 4, Murcia ☎ 968 21 55 79 🕐 Lunch and dinner

There's plenty of choice of hotels, from beachside towers in and around Benidorm to boutiques, rural retreats and *pensiones*.

Introduction

The cheapest accommodation is all-inclusive options booked before arrival, though a small town hotel can be almost as cheap and you can be sure your money is all going to local people.

Location

Benidorm and nearby Altea are the most popular places to stay and offer the most hotels. But here you are immersed more in British and Northern European culture. Those looking for a more local experience opt either for a hotel on the beach in Alicante or in the Spanish resorts like Gandia or Jávea. It is also possible to stay in the pretty Moorish towns in the hills, which are only a short drive from the beaches. There are increasing numbers of smart converted farmhouse hotels and hotels.

Types of accommodation

Spanish hotels are classified on a star system which ranges from one to five stars (with a deluxe category of *Gran Lujo*, GL). While this can be a useful guideline it groups the hotels according to their facilities, size, price and numbers of services. These are based on a checklist: is there a restaurant; is there a lift; are there business facilities? The more ticks in the boxes, the higher the rating. However the star system does not reflect quality, charm, decoration, location or ambience. Family-run *pensiones* can often be more comfortable and offer better services than the equivalent and higher star-rated hotels. It is also possible to rent a villa or farmhouse on the Costa Blanca. These are almost invariably self-catering.

Hotel in Mar Menor; Huerto del Cura Hotel, Elche; poolside in Benidorm; high-rise hotels dominate Benidorm

DISABLED ACCESS

While they have a long way to go, facilities for travellers with disabilities are improving. Although ground floor rooms are rare, most larger hotels have parking, wheelchair access and lifts. In resort areas and large towns there are usually ramps to the beaches. Remoter areas have few facilities. Contact Fedarcion Ecom ✉ Gran Via de les Corts Catalanes 562, Barcelona; www.ecom.es

Budget Hotels

PRICES

Expect to pay up to €100 per night for a double room in a budget hotel.

COSTA BLANCA CAMPING

www.campingcostablanca.com
Spacious bungalows and a large, well-equipped campsite a kilometre (0.6 miles) from the beach between the port area and the Playa del Puerto Español. Facilties include a kids' organized activity area, laundry, large pool, gym and bar/restaurant.
🔲 Off map at f1 ✉ Calle Convento 143, Alicante ☎ 965 63 06 70

HOSTAL CANDILEJAS

www.hostalcandilejas.com
The rooms may be small, plain and simple but all are spruce and have bathrooms and this friendly little guest house is in a good location right in the heart of the Elche's historic centre.
🔲 G4 ✉ Calle Doctor Ferran 19, Elche ☎ 965 46 65 12

HOTEL ALAMEDA

www.hotelalameda.es
This small, spruce three-star hotel offers one of the best deals in Benidorm. It's in a good location on the north side of the old town with easy access to both beaches and is very popular with Spanish couples.
🔲 K5 ✉ Calle Alameda 34, Benidorm ☎ 965 85 56 50

HOTEL CERVANTES

www.hotel-cervantes.es
Thirty simple but well-kept rooms in a little tower hotel in the commercial centre. The waterfront and castle are both less than ten minutes' walk away and the hotel has a little ground-floor café serving pastries and thick, strong Spanish coffee from breakfast until the small hours.
🔲 d4 ✉ Calle Médico Pascual Pérez 19 at Calle Navas, Alicante ☎ 965 20 98 22

LA HUERTANICA

www.hotellahuertanica.com
It may have small, simple rooms but staff in this guest house are warm and friendly and it's convenient for the cathedral and tiny streets and alleys of Murcia's city centre.
🔲 j3 ✉ Calle Infantes 3–5, Murcia ☎ 968 21 76 68

GREEN VISITS

Although it is widely touted by the local mayor as an ecotourism destination for its clean beaches and low-energy street lighting, Benidorm's size and industrial-strength tourism means that it still falls wide of the mark. And with its vilified environmental record, Murcia is one of the worst ecotourism destinations in Spain—especially for buying a home. But there are options for the green traveller (▷ panels 110, 111).

LOS RAYOS DEL SOL

www.alteabedandbreakfast.com
A big faux-art deco hacienda in the hills some 10km (6 miles) north of Altea, with magnificent views of the coast and surrounding mountains from the terrace, a range of simple, functional rooms and a full (English) breakfast.
🔲 K5 ✉ Carrer Mar de Alborán 10, La Nucia, Altea ☎ 697 42 77 11

RESIDENCIA BRISTOL

www.onasol.es
This town house hotel in the heart of the old town is pretty much the cheapest option in Benidorm. Rooms are small and very simple but both beaches are less than ten minutes' walk away and there are plenty of budget restaurants and café bars close by.
🔲 K5 ✉ Calle Martínez Alejos 1, Benidorm ☎ 966 80 53 59

SAN REMO

www.hotelsanremo.net
Modest but very well run little town hotel in a good location close to the castle and two blocks from the seafront. En suite rooms are spruce in tile and white paint, have cable TV and the best have balconies. WiFi internet access in reception.
🔲 d4 ✉ Calle Navas 30 at Calle del Teatro, Alicante ☎ 965 20 95 00

Mid-Range Hotels

PRICES

Expect to pay between €100–€200 per night for a double room in a mid-range hotel.

ALMIRANTE

www.hotelalmirante.com
There are great sea views from this hotel in the city's San Juan district—the best location for windsurfing and water sports enthusiasts. The hotel has a decent restaurant.
✚ Off map at f1 ✉ Avenida Niza 38, Playa de San Juan, Alicante ☎ 965 65 01 12

BARCELÓ ASIA GARDENS

www.asiagardens.es
Set in striking gardens, the balconies at this Asian-style designed hotel have splendid views out over Benidorm's skyline and the beaches and blue sea beyond. All rooms are bright and decked out in marble with thick bed linen and frowsty business hotel furniture. But you'll need to drive 5 minutes to reach the beach.
✚ K5 ✉ Avenida Eduardo Zaplana s/n, Glorieta del Fuego ☎ 966 81 84 00

CASA GENOVEVA

www.casagenoveva.es
A fully equipped and restored turn of the century rural farmhouse set in the countryside 2km (1 mile) from Relleu village—in the hills 20km (12 miles) northeast of Benidorm. A great option for a family or couple looking for a quiet retreat in easy driving distance of the coastal beaches and cities.
✚ K5 ✉ Partida Muscaret s/n, Relleu, Benidorm ☎ 965 86 36 34

CASA LEHMI

www.casalehmi.com
This gorgeous, restored country mansion about 10km (6 miles) from Guadalest is surrounded by maquis-covered hills and offers a self-consciously quiet, back to Naure rural retreat from the hedonism of the coast, that promises to 'get your daily life in perspective'. Rooms and public areas are beautifully appointed and the hotel can organize activities from walks to horse rides.
✚ K4 ✉ El Buscarró 1–3, Tárbena, Alicante ☎ 965 88 40 18

RESPONSIBLE TRAVEL

www.responsibletravel.com offer 7-night guided walking and nature holidays in the region staying in locally owned accommodation, and operators like ethical escape http://ethicalescape.com have options nearby. www.discoveringcartagena.com/environment.htm have volunteer environmental programmes in Murcia.

CASTILLA ALICANTE

www.alicantehotelcastilla.com
Large, modern hotel block a few hundred metres from the beach in San Juan, with balcony rooms, a pool shaded by palms and an efficient English-speaking reception able to book everything from car rentals to tours. Breakfast is included in the price.
✚ Off map at f1 ✉ Avenida Países Escandinavos 7, Playa de San Juan, Alicante ☎ 965 16 20 33

FLEMING

www.onasol.es
A family-friendly salmon pink concrete block 150m (155 yards) from Playa Poniente popular with Spanish holiday-makers. Rooms are small but bright, have cable TV and terraced balconies and there's a pool.
✚ K5 ✉ Calle Maravall at Campana, Benidorm ☎ 965 85 32 62

HOTEL BILBAINO

www.hotelbilbaino.com
This family-run hotel has been here since Benidorm was a sleepy village and it retains a privileged location overlooking the beach, without charging as highly as some of the larger, more modern complexes. The sea-front rooms are a particularly good deal out of season.
✚ K5 ✉ Avenida Virgen de Sufragio 1, Benidorm ☎ 965 85 08 04 or 965 85 08 05

HOTEL L'ESTACIO

www.hotelestacio.com
Another tastefully appointed, quiet, relaxing country retreat—set in wooded gardens near the Sierra Mariola. Rooms are understated and decked out with a mix of modern luxurious and chunky rustic furniture. The public areas include a sitting room with comfy sofas and a log fire, and there is a beautiful sunny terrace, too.

➕ K2 ✉ Parc de L'Estació, Bocairent, Valencia ☎ 962 35 00 00

HOTEL RIO PARK

www.medplaya.com
Thomson Holidays' popular good-value hotel in Benidorm is a towering high-rise four blocks from the beach watching over a large swimming pool. Rooms are spacious and all have balconies. The reception can organize everything from tours to car hire. Very good internet rates are available.

➕ K5 ✉ Calle Murcia 16, Benidorm ☎ 965 85 56 12

JAIME 1

www.hoteljaimebenidorm.com
This is one of the smaller, quieter hotels in Benidorm—200m (220 yards) from the beach and in easy walking distance of all the nightlife. It's popular with the Spanish and was fully refurbished in 2002.

➕ K5 ✉ Avenida Jaime I 11, Benidorm ☎ 965 85 07 19

MEDITERRANEA PLAZA

www.eurostars.com
This is one of the best hotels in Alicante's old centre. Large doubles come with plush bathrooms and there are decent business services. In easy walking distance of the castle, port and Postiguet beach.

➕ e4 ✉ Plaza del Ayuntamiento 6, Alicante ☎ 965 21 01 88

MONT SANT

www.hosteriamontsant.com
For stays as close as possible to Jativa's magnificent castle head for this converted finca hideaway secreted in its own pine wood and palm gardens just below the battlement walls. Rooms are rural chic with rough hewn drystone walls, rich, heavy bed linen and gorgeous views from the private balconies. The restaurant is one of the region's finest.

➕ L2 ✉ Subida al Castillo s/n, Jativa ☎ 962 27 50 81

NH ALICANTE

www.nh-hotels.com
There are wonderful panoramic views of the castle and waterfront from this modern minimalist hotel in the heart of Alicante's shopping district. Facilities are excellent—with a well-equipped gym, sauna, business centre and a very good restaurant. But there is no pool.

➕ Off map at a4 ✉ Calle Mexico 18 at Rosa Chacel, Alicante ☎ 965 10 81 40

ROCA ESMERALDA

www.rocaesmeralda.com
A monolithic concrete hotel with an array of indoor and outdoor pools, restaurants and booking agencies, watching over the beach and the rock in central Calpe. Rooms are modern, smart and come with large terraces all with a beach view.

➕ L5 ✉ Playa Levante, Calpe ☎ 902 99 65 69

SPA PORTA MARIS

www.hotelspaportamaris.com
This hotel sits in Alicante's refurbished waterfront area just south of the castle. All the well-appointed, spacious suites have sea views—as does the restaurant. The spa is the best in central Alicante and there are excellent business facilities.

➕ e4 ✉ Plaza Puerta del Mar 3, Alicante ☎ 965 14 70 21

Luxury Hotels

PRICES

Expect to pay over €200 per night for a double room in a luxury hotel.

ARCO DE SAN JUAN

www.arcosanjuan.com

The best hotel in Murcia's city centre is housed in a restored 18th-century neoclassical palace a stone's throw from the cathedral. Services include one of Murcia's best restaurants.

➕ j3 ✉ Plaza Ceballos 10, Murcia ☎ 968 21 04 55

HOSPES AMERIGO

www.hospes.com

The finest hotel in Alicante is in a refurbished Dominican convent next to the town hall and a stroll from the beach. It's the only five-star in the centre.

➕ d4 ✉ Calle Rafael Altamira 7, Alicante ☎ 965 14 65 70

HOTEL BALI

www.granhotelbali.com

This enormous modern tower together with its neighbours has contributed to transforming Benidorm's skyline into a Mediterranean Vegas. Facilities are on a grand scale—with a choice of pools, a spa, gym and extensive conference facilities. But it's not for lovers of quiet.

➕ K5 ✉ Calle Luis Prendes s/n, Benidorm ☎ 966 81 52 00

EL MONTÍBOLI

www.hotelelmontiboli.com

A superior spa hotel in the Relais et Chateaux group with a superior view from a rocky promontory out over two twin talcum powder fine beaches and the Mediterranean. The hotel restaurant is excellent.

➕ K5 ✉ Partida Montíboli s/n, Villajoyosa ☎ 965 90 02 50

PALÁCIO DE TUDEMIR

www.solmelia.com

One of the region's finest hotels housed in a tastefully restored Renaissance mansion in the centre close to the cathedral and historic buildings. Facilities and service are first class.

➕ F4 ✉ Calle Alfonso XIII 1, Orihuela ☎ 966 73 80 10

PARADOR DE JÁVEA

www.parador.es

This and Puerto Lumbreras (▷ below) are the only Paradors on the Costa Blanca and this is the only one on the beach. The main building is a large concrete affair overlooking the sea and offering rooms with splendid Mediterranean views. The restaurant and service are excellent.

➕ M5 ✉ Avenida del Mediterráneo 223, Jávea ☎ 965 79 02 00

PARADOR PUERTO LUMBRERAS

www.parador.es

A large town house 30km (19 miles) from the coast converted into a luxury parador hotel. The rooms are simple but elegant, there's a play area for children in the hotel garden, a large pool and a superb restaurant serving local dishes. The hotel is about 15km (7.5 miles) from Murcia city. Prices are surprisingly good.

➕ B3 ✉ Avenida Juan Carlos I 77, Puerto Lumbreras, Murcia ☎ 968 40 20 25

VILLAITANA WELLNESS, GOLF AND BUSINESS RESORT

www.villaitana.com

This is Benidorm's most luxurious hotel with accommodation laid out in a mock Mediterranean village with its own artificial beach, spa, wonderful views out over the city and two golf courses. There are complimentary transfers to the beach.

➕ K5 ✉ Avenida de Alcalde Eduardo Zaplana Hérnandez-Soro 7, Benidorm ☎ 966 81 50 00

SPAS

Natural hot springs have been used in Fortuna in Murcia since Roman times and the spa there—in the old-fashioned sense of the word—remains popular today. There are modern luxury spas too, in most of the larger hotels; check out the Villaitana Golf and Business Resort (▷ this page).

There are direct, economical flights to
the Costa Blanca from the rest of Europe
and there are bus and train connections
between the main centres in the region
but the only way to remoter locations is
with a rental car.

Planning Ahead

When to Go

It is warm and sunny all year round on the Costa Blanca. Spring and early summer are the best times to visit, when the temperatures are at their balmiest. Mid-summer temperatures can reach 34°C (93°F). Crowds are at their thinnest in late autumn, winter and early spring.

TIME

L Spain is six hours ahead of New York, nine hours ahead of Los Angeles and one hour ahead of the UK.

AVERAGE DAILY MAXIMUM TEMPERATURES

JAN	FEB	MAR	APR	MAY	JUN	JUL	AUG	SEP	OCT	NOV	DEC
62°F	66°F	66°F	70°F	75°F	82°F	82°F	93°F	84°F	80°F	70°F	64°F
17°C	19°C	19°C	21°C	24°C	28°C	28°C	34°C	29°C	27°C	21°C	18°C

Spring (March to May) Mostly balmy and pleasant with clear skies, but occasional thunderstorms or light rain.
Summer (May to September) Hot, and in July and August dry. Crowds are at their peak in this period.
Autumn (October to November) The wettest months but still warm and with a fair chance of sunshine.
Winter (December to February) Cool and sometimes wet in December, but with a greater chance of bright and clear skies in January and February.

WHAT'S ON

January
6 January *Los Reyes Magos* (Twelfth Night/Adoration of the Magi): marked with street parades celebrating the arrival of the three wise men at Jesus's crib. Christmas gifts are given to children in Spanish families.
February/March
Mardi Gras: carnival to celebrate the beginning of Lent.
March/April
Semana Santa and *La Pasqua* (Holy Week and Easter): costumed street parades bearing Catholic effigies commemorate the events of Christ's Passion and culminate with joyous

celebrations on Easter Sunday. The best are in Cartagena, Jumilla, Murcia, Moratalla, Orihuela, Alicante and Elche. There is also an Easter pilgrimage to Santa Fez monastery in Alicante attended by some 100,000 faithful.
Moros y Cristianos: festivals celebrating the Reconquest of Moorish southern Spain by the crusader kings of Aragon and Castile, a costumed pageant with street parades and concerts. The largest is in Alcoy.
June
Hogueras de San Juan: a week-long mid-summer festival in Alicante with

parades, bull fights and firework displays.
August
Misteri d'Elx: a series of processions and musical events and a long mystery play celebrate the Assumption of Our Lady in Elche.
Festival Nacional del Cante de las Minas: an important flamenco festival taking place in Murcia.
December
31 December *Víspera del Año Nuevo* (New Year's Eve): 12 grapes—one for each chime of the clock—are eaten on the toll of midnight to break in the new year.

Useful Websites

http://costablanca.comunitatvalenciana.com
The official Valencia government tourism site
for the region in English, French, German,
Chinese, Japanese and Spanish but not
Portuguese.

www.murciaturistica.es
Official tourism site of the Murcia government
in English, French, German and Spanish.

www.benidorm-spotlight.com
www.benidorm.to
Comprehensive information on the Costa
Blanca's entertainment capital with maps,
entertainment, restaurants and tours.

www.costa-news.com
An English-language online newspaper on the
Costa Blanca.

www.infocostablanca.com
Reliable overview information with maps for
the entire region.

www.alicanteturismo.com
A comprehensive and practical site about
Alicante and the surrounding area, including
attractions, activities, festivals. shopping, excursions, accommodation, restaurants and more.

www.costablancauncovered.com
A catch-all portal in English and German for all
things Costa Blanca from holidays to homes
abroad. Aimed at the mainstream tourist.

www.idealspain.com
One of the best overall sites on Spain with
a comprehensive range of information on
everything from football to fiestas and music
and culture to a complete list of Spanish castles
with a potted run-down of their history.

TRAVEL SITE

www.fodors.com
Excellent information and
travel-planning site with
reliable indications of price
and weather.

www.spain.info
Spain's official website with a
wealth of visual and practical
information about the entire
country and plenty on the
Costa Blanca.

CYBERCAFÉS

Even the cheapest hotels
tend to have an internet
terminal or WiFi.
Below are two cybercafés:

Arroba
✉ Calle La Fuente 3b,
Totana, Murcia
☎ 968 42 43 32

Bemay
✉ Calle Lepanto 9,
Benidorm
☎ 965 85 52 29

Getting There

VISITORS WITH DISABILITIES

General access on the Costa Blanca is poor—as it is in the rest of Spain. Only a fraction of taxis and buses have disabled access and most museums and attractions do not provide ramps for disabled access. But things are improving. The new tourist sights are generally fitted with disabled access and facilities and Alicante and Benidorm in particular are making concerted efforts. There is now disabled access all the way up to Alicante castle, for example, both by lift and ramps. English language advice is available from www.access-able.com. FAMMA is the Spanish association dealing with disabilities—www.famma.org.

API

Non-EU passengers on all flights entering Spain are required to supply Advanced Passenger Information (API) to the Spanish Police before travelling. This comprises name, nationality, date of birth and document number. The information is usually submitted by travel agents or airline check-in staff.

AIRPORTS

There are three main gateways to the Costa Blanca. Alicante is the most popular with the greatest choice of international flights at the best prices. There is also an airport at Murcia with connections to the rest of Spain. Valencia is another point of entry.

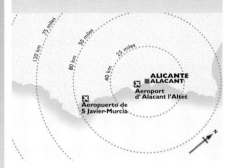

ALICANTE ▪ALACANT
Aeroport d' Alacant l'Altet

Aeropuerto de S Javier-Murcia

BY AIR

Spain's national carrier Iberia (www.iberia. com) ☎ 902 40 05 00 has flights to Alicante's l'Altet airport (10km/6 miles from town) and to Valencia's Manises airport (15km/9 miles from town). There are taxi stands and local and international car rental companies in both airports. A taxi to Alicante city centre from the airport (journey time 15 minutes) costs about €17–€22.

Low cost airlines such as EasyJet (www. easyjet.com), Ryan Air (www.ryanair.com) and Monarch (www.flymonarch.com) fly direct to Alicante from various UK and northern European airports. There are often restrictions or even charges for hold luggage and the in flight service is very limited—especially Ryan Air. Scheduled airlines like British Airways (www.ba.com) and Iberia (www.iberia.com) are more expensive but service and luggage allowances are markedly better.

Flights from North America go via Madrid and take between six and seven hours from the US

Eastern seaboard. Iberia (in the US ☎ 800 772 4642) offer some of the best deals and have the best onward connections to the Costa Blanca and anywhere else in Spain. They have daily non-stop flights between Madrid and New York, Chicago and Miami, and also offer fly-drive packages. Air Europa (US ☎ 888 238 7672, www.air-europa.com) have a non-stop service JFK to Madrid with onward connections to Alicante or Valencia. American (www.aa.com) fly to Madrid from JFK, Boston and Miami, Delta (www.delta.com) to Madrid and Barcelona from Atlanta, Cincinatti, LA, Salt Lake City and JFK, Continental (www.continental.com) to Madrid from Newark and US Airways (www.usairways.com) to Madrid from Philadelphia and Dallas. You will need to buy onward connections to the Costa Blanca with one of the above or with Spanair (www.spanair.com) or take a train.

BY TRAIN
Renfe (www.renfe.es) have at least seven trains per day running between Madrid and Alicante. The journey takes three and a half hours and costs around €70. From Barcelona there are at least five trains per day, the journey takes five hours and costs around €50.

BY BOAT
There are ferries across the Mediterranean to Oran in Algeria, North Africa from Alicante (www.trasmediterranea.es) or (www.sncm.fr).

CUSTOMS REGULATIONS
The limits for non-EU visitors over 18 (including those who arrive from outside the EU) are 200 cigarettes or 50 cigars, or 250g of raw tobacoo, 1 litre of spirits, 2 of liquor or wine and 50ml of perfume. EU residents are entitled to 800 cigarettes, 200 cigars, 1kg of tobacco, 10 litres of spirits, 20 of fortified wine, 90 of wine and 110 of beer.

ENTRY REQUIREMENTS
Only a valid passport is required by members of other EU states, Norway, Iceland and Switzerland. Australians and New Zealanders, Canadians, Israelis, and people from the US do not require a visa for stays less than 90 days. Citizens of other countries must apply for a visa in person before arriving in Spain. Any non-EU resident wishing to stay in Spain for longer than 90 days require a residence card (*tarjeta de residencia*).

INSURANCE
Some travellers choose to take out travel insurance to cover possible loss of baggage and healthcare while abroad. Spain has excellent medical facilities.

TIP
● For more information including contact numbers and car hire see www.spanish-airport-guide.com.

Getting Around

CAR RENTAL

Cars offer the most convenience on the Costa Blanca. The large car-rental firms are represented in the airports and in the major town centre. But it is best to book from home either on the web or via an agent. It will work out at a fraction of the standard Spanish airport price. Small cars are best for the mountain roads and the environment.

CONCESSIONS

Many museums and attractions offer concessions to students, senior citizens (aged over 60) and people with disablities. Students should bring an international student card (ISIC: www.isic.org) or a Euro 26 (www.euro26.org) card with them.

CAR RENTAL

● Car rental is available at both Alicante's El Altet airport and at Valencia's Manises airport. It is essential to book in advance during the peak summer period. Expect to wait at least an hour to get your car when the airport is at its busiest.
● Book through
Europcar (www.europcar.com)
Hertz (www.hertz.com)
Avis (www.avis.com) and most other large rental companies.

DRIVING

● Driving is on the right-hand side in Spain.
● The speed limit on motorways (*autopistas*) is 120kph.
● The speed limit on dual carriageways is 100kph and on country highways 90kph.
● There is extensive random breath testing and speed cameras are widespread.
● Seatbelts must be worn in the front seat for all journeys.

● Unleaded fuel (*gasolina*) is available as Super plus (98 octane) and Super (96 octane). Diesel (*gasoleo* or *gasoil*) is sold though not as widely as in other European countries and there are few diesel-fuelled cars.
● Fuel stations are usually open between 6am and10pm and later or even 24 hours on the large motorways and toll roads. Credit cards are usually accepted.

TAXIS
● Taxi ranks are marked with a blue square with a T inside it and are widespread in the larger cities and towns.
● Cabs with a green light or a *libre* (free) placard can also be flagged down in the street. They can legally carry only four passengers.
● Tariff lists are posted at taxi ranks.

TRAINS
The Costa Blanca has two railways.
● Renfe have a fast service on broad gauge running between the principal cities, Madrid and Barcelona.
● The Alicante-Dénia narrow-gauge line is a slower but more scenic route along the coastline, stopping at almost every one of the 40 stations along the way. It is operated by FGV (☎ 965 26 22 33; www.fgv.es) from a seperate station on Avenida Villajoyosa, Alicante.

BUSES
● Alicante is the principal hub. The bus station (☎ 965 13 07 00) is on Calle Portugal and has services running to most of the major towns in the Costa Blanca region. There are hourly services along the coast. Tickets are numbered and must be bought in advance.
● Murcia's bus station in on Calle Sierra Nevada (☎ 968 29 22 11).

BOATS
● Illa de Tabarca (▷ 32–33), the principal island of a rocky archipelago south of the Costa Blanca, can be reached from Alicante, Santa Pola or Torrevieja between April and November.
● Excursions allow a full day on the island and can be booked through
Kon Tiki ☎ 965 21 63 96
Barco Santa Pola a Tabarca ☎ 965 41 11 13
Cruceros Tabardo ☎ 966 70 21 22

MAPS
● Basic maps are available at most tourist offices (▷ 121).

ORGANIZED SIGHTSEEING
The tourist offices in Alicante and Benidorm have lists of tour operators offering excursions around the towns, and most hotels can help with similar tours.
● Viator (www.viator.com) are an international web-based company who allow you to book a huge range of tours in and around the Costa Blanca whilst there or before leaving your home country. Trips include jeep safaris in the Sierra, catamaran cruises along the coast, visits to the theme parks and walks around the cities, including Alicante.
● Spain is serious about its cycling and has produced several Tour de France champions. The Costa Blanca is a popular training ground for sports cyclists. Sporting tours (www.sportingtours. co.uk) offer trips around the region for serious cyclists. Tuk Tuk (www.tuktuktours. co.uk) offer tours off the beaten track in the northern Costa Blanca beginning in Jávea.

Essential Facts

CONSULATES

- UK ☎ 965 21 60 22
- USA ☎ 932 80 22 27
- Netherlands ☎ 965 21 21 75
- Germany ☎ 965 21 70 27

MONEY

The official currency in Spain is the euro–introduced in 2002. This is divided into note denominations of 5, 10, 20, 50, 100, 200 and 500. Coins come in 2, 5, 10, 20 and 50 cents and 1 and 2 euros.

€5

€10

€20

€50

BUSINESS HOURS

- Standard opening hours for shops are Mon-Sat 9.30am–1.30pm, closed for siesta and then 4.30pm–8pm, closed on Sundays.
- Large stores usually stay open all day from 10am–9pm. Many businesses including restaurants and bars (especially in Madrid) close in August.
- Banks usually operate to standard European hours Mon–Fri 9am–4pm.

ELECTRICITY

- The power supply is 220–225 volts ac in standard European two-pin, round-socket plugs. A transformer is needed for apparatus operating on 110–120 volts and an adaptor for US and UK plugs. Bring a universal adaptor (available in most airports) with you as they are not easy to find on the Costa Blanca.

MEDICINE

- Spanish medicine compares favourably in price with the rest of Europe.
- Many UK prescription medicines are available over the counter.

MONEY

- ATMs (cashpoints) are widely distributed throughout the Costa Blanca and accept Mastercard and Visa. A few will also take Amex.
- Traveller's cheques can be cashed at most banks and *casas de cambio* (exchange booths) though they may incur a fee.
- Foreign currency can also be exchanged at banks and *casas de cambio*.

RELIGION

- Over 98 per cent of people are Catholic.
- Significant others are Protestants, Muslims and Jewish.

TELEPHONES

- To make an international call from Spain, dial 00 and then add the country code:
UK 44

Republic of Ireland 353
USA & Canada 1
Australia 61
France 33
Germany 49
Netherlands 31
Portugal 351

TOURIST INFORMATION OFFICES
● Alicante
✉ Rambla Méndez Núñez 23
Alicante 03002
☎ 965 20 00 00; www.costablanca.org

● Benidorm
✉ Avenida Martinez Alejos 16
Benidorm 03501
☎ 965 85 13 11; www.benidorm.org

● Elche
✉ Plaça de Parc 3
Paseo de la Estácion, Elche 03203
☎ 966 65 81 95; www.turismedelx.com

Orihuela
● ✉ Palácio del Marqués de Rubalcava
Calle Francisco Díe 25, Orihuela 03300
☎ 965 30 27 47; www.aytoorihuela.com

USEFUL TELEPHONE NUMBERS
● Directory assistance ☎ 118 22
● Operator ☎ 118 22
● Toll-free ☎ 900
● Emergency services ☎ 112
● Ambulance/Ambulancia ☎ 061
● Fire service/Bombers/Bomberos ☎ 080
● National Police/Policia Nacional ☎ 091 (for serious trouble)
● Municipal Police/Policia Municipal ☎ 092 (for larger towns and cities)
● Civil Guard/Guardia Civil ☎ 062 (for smaller towns and villages)

TIME DIFFERENCES
● GMT 12 noon
● Spain 1pm
● Germany 1pm
● France 1pm
● NYC 7am
● Miami 7am
● Los Angeles 5am

TOURIST OFFICES
● In the UK
✉ Turespaña, 2nd floor, 79 New Cavendish Street, London W1W 6XB
☎ 020 7317 2010
www.spain.info/uk/tourspain

● In the USA
✉ Tourist Office of Spain, 35th floor, 666 5th Avenue New York, NY 10103
☎ 212 265 8822
www.spain.info/us/tourspain

● In Canada
✉ Spain National Tourist Office
2 Bloor St W, Suite 3402 Toronto, Ontario M4W 3E2
☎ 416 961 3131
www.spain.info/ca/tourspain

NEED TO KNOW ESSENTIAL FACTS

Language

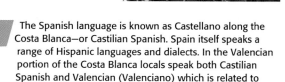

The Spanish language is known as Castellano along the Costa Blanca—or Castilian Spanish. Spain itself speaks a range of Hispanic languages and dialects. In the Valencian portion of the Costa Blanca locals speak both Castilian Spanish and Valencian (Valenciano) which is related to Catalan. In Murcia they speak Castilian—with some regional variations in accents and slang. English is widely spoken in and around Benidorm but will be little understood elsewhere.

BASIC VOCABULARY

good morning	*buenos dias*
good afternoon/ evening	*buenas tardes*
good night	*buenas noches*
hello (informal)	*hola*
goodbye (informal)	*hasta luego/hasta pronto*
hello (on the phone)	*¿Diga?*
goodbye	*adios*
please	*por favor*
thank you	*gracias*
you're welcome	*de nada*
how are you? (formal)	*¿Cómo está?*
how are you? (informal)	*¿Que tal?*
I'm fine	*estoy bien*
I'm sorry	*lo siento*
excuse me	*perdón*
I don't understand	*no entiendo*
I don't speak Spanish	*no hablo español*
how much is it?	*¿cuanto es?*
where is the…?	*¿dónde está…?*
do you have…?	*¿tiene…?*
I'd like…	*me gustaría*
I don't know	*No lo sé*
It doesn't matter	*No importa*
How much/many?	*¿Cuánto/cuántos?*
Is/are there?	*¿Hay?*

USEFUL WORDS

yes	*sí*
no	*no*
Where?	*¿Dónde?*
When?	*¿Cuándo?*
Why?	*¿Por qué?*
What?	*¿Que?*
Who?	*¿Quién?*
How?	*¿Cómo?*
ticket	*entrada*
big	*grande*
small	*pequeño*
with	*con*
without	*sin*
hot	*caliente*
cold	*frío*
early	*temprano*
late	*tarde*
here	*aquí*
there	*alli*
today	*hoy*
tomorrow	*mañana*
yesterday	*ayer*
menu	*la carta*
entrance	*entrada*
exit	*salida*
open	*abierto*
closed	*cerrado*
good	*bueno*
bad	*malo*

MONEY

bank	*banco*
exchange office	*oficina de cambio*
coin	*moneda*
money	*dinero*
cheque	*cheque*
traveller's cheque	*cheque de viajero*
credit card	*tarjeta de crédito*
bank card	*tarjeta del banco*
change money	*cambiar dinero*
cashier	*cajero*
foreign currency	*moneda extranjero*

TRANSPORTATION

aeroplane/airport	*avion/aeropuerto*
train	*tren*
bus	*autobús*
car	*coche*
ticket	*billette*
seat	*asiento*

HOTELS

hotel	*hotel*
single room	*habitación individual*
double room	*habitación doble*
one person	*una persona*
one night	*una noche*
reservation	*reservacíon*
bath	*baño*
shower	*ducha*
toilet	*lavabo*
key	*llave*
lift	*ascensor*
balcony	*balcón*
sea view	*vista al mar*
chambermaid	*camarera*
breakfast	*desayuno*

EATING OUT

café	*café*
pub/bar	*bar*
breakfast	*desayuno*
lunch	*almuerzo*
dinner	*cena*
waiter	*camarero*
waitress	*camerera*
starter	*primer plato*
main course	*plato principal*
dessert	*postre*
bill	*cuenta*
beer	*cervesa*
wine	*vino*
water	*agua*
table	*mesa*
coffee	*café*

Timeline

Neanderthal and Paleolithic cave dwelling people who probably migrated from North Africa settled throughout the Iberian peninsula and left their mark on caves throughout Spain and Portugal—most famously in Altamira and the Coa Valley in Portugal.

5000 BC Agriculture develops. During the Bronze Age the Celts arrive and settle Iberia. Urban cultures develop.

1000 BC Phoenicians and Greeks establish trading ports along the Spanish coast including around Alicante and Cartagena.

264 BC The Carthaginian Empire stretches to southern Spain. Cartagena becomes a major Carthaginian city.

218–201 BC Hannibal from Játiva nearly conquers Rome for the Carthaginians in the Second Punic War.

200 BC Romans establish major port towns at Dénia, Alicante and Cartagena.

AD 100–500 Christianity arrives in Spain. The Vandals establish strong colonies in Vandalusia (Andalusia) and along the Costa Blanca. They later become Romanized.

711 Arabs arrive in Iberia and establish an enlightened and progressive civilization based from Al-Andalus.

711–1200 The Arabs modernize Spain, introducing progressive systems of agriculture. Jews, Chrisitans and Muslims live harmoniously in the Moorish cities under a floresence of intellectual culture that produces some of Europe's finest thinkers, including Averroes who introduces Aristotle's thought to Europe,

From left to right: Hannibal; Moorish windows in Calaforra tower, Elche; Moorish stronghold of La Atalaya dominates the town on Villena; Murcia's cathedral entrance; castle walls at Moraira; Napoleon Bonaparte; the Benidorm coastline

Maimonides and the writers of the great mystical book of Judaism—the Zohar.

1200–1300 The beginnings of the brutal Reconquest. Much of Murcia is taken by Jaime of Aragon. Alicante falls in 1248. The kingdom of Valencia is founded in 1244. Murcia becomes a trading post with neighbouring Moorish Andalucia.

1400–1700 Spain unites as one country in 1492 under the union of Ferdinand of Aragon and Sicily and Isabella of Castile. The final expulsion of the Moors begins along with the brutal Inquisition under which Muslims and Jews are forced to convert or face execution.

1701–14 Spain is ravaged by the War of the Spanish Succession.

1808–14 Napoleon's Peninsular campaign destroys Spanish influence.

1936–39 Spanish Civil War and the establishment of fascism under Franco.

1960s Mass tourism begins in Benidorm.

1975 Franco dies and Spain enters the late 20th century as a fledgling democracy.

1986 Spain joins the EU.

2009 Elections for Presidency of European Commission.

MUSLIM RULE

Murcia and Valencia were under Muslim rule for more than 500 years. The structure of the cities and villages throughout modern Costa Blanca remain Moorish. The Arabs introduced irrigation, decorative abstract art, sophisticated mathematics, the ideas of Aristotle and modern military techniques—paving the way for the rise of Spanish imperial power and the conquest of the Americas in the centuries after the Reconquest in 1248 by Jaime the Conqueror.

MOORS AND CHRISTIANS

The Costa Blanca celebrates the Reconquest in more than 80 different towns and villages, with costumed processions and mock battles. The most spectacular is in Alcoy (22–24 April) when thousands of locals dressed-up as different Christian and Muslim factions descend on the town's main plaza for a spectacular firework display.

Index

TWINPACK
Costa Blanca

WRITTEN BY Alex Robinson
VERIFIED BY Lindsay Bennett and Penny Phenix
COVER DESIGN Jacqueline Bailey
DESIGN WORK Bookwork Creative Associates Ltd
INDEXER Marie Lorimer
IMAGE RETOUCHING AND REPRO Sarah Montgomery, Michael Moody and James Tims
PROJECT EDITOR Bookwork Creative Associates Ltd
SERIES EDITOR Cathy Harrison

© AA MEDIA LIMITED 2010

Colour separation by AA Digital Department
Printed and bound by Leo Paper Products, China

A CIP catalogue record for this book is available from the British Library.

ISBN 978-0-7495-6148-2

Published by AA Publishing, a trading name of AA Media Limited, whose registered office is Fanum House, Basing View, Basingstoke, Hampshire RG21 4EA. Registered number 06112600.

Front cover image: AA/M Chaplow
Back cover images: (i) and (iii) AA/M Chaplow; (ii) AA/C Sawyer
(iv) AA/J Edmanson

A03639
Maps in this title produced from mapping © MAIRDUMONT / Falk Verlag 2010

The Automobile Association would like to thank the following photographers, companies and picture libraries for their assistance in the preparation of this book.

Abbreviations for the pictures credits are as follows – (t) top; (b) bottom; (c) centre; (l) left; (r) right; (AA) AA World Travel Library.

1 AA/M Chaplow; 2–18 top panel AA/M Chaplow; 4 AA/M Chaplow; 5 AA/M Chaplow; 6tl AA/M Chaplow; 6tc AA/J Edmanson; 6tr AA/M Chaplow; 6bl Brand X Pics; 6bc AA/C Sawyer; 6br AA/C Sawyer; 7tl AA/M Chaplow; 7tc AA/M Langford; 7tr AA/M Chaplow; 7bl AA/M Chaplow; 7bc AA/M Chaplow; 7br AA/M Chaplow; 10t AA/S Watkins; 10c(i) AA/M Chaplow; 10c(ii) AA/M Chaplow; 10b AA/M Chaplow; 11t(i) AA/M Chaplow; 11t(ii) AA/M Chaplow; 11c(ii) AA/M Chaplow; 11c(ii) AA/M Chaplow; 11b AA/M Chaplow; 12t AA/M Chaplow; 12c(i) AA/J Edmanson; 12c(ii) AA/J Tims; 12b AA/M Chaplow; 13t(i) AA/M Chaplow; 13t(ii) AA/C Sawyer; 13c(i) AA/C Sawyer; 13c(ii) Digitalvision; 13b AA/J Edmanson; 14t AA/M Chaplow; 14c(i) AA/C Sawyer; 14c(ii) Imagestate; 14b AA/K Paterson; 15 AA/M Chaplow; 16t AA/M Chaplow; 16c(i) AA/M Chaplow; 16c(ii) Courtesy of Fundación MARQ; 16b AA/J Edmanson; 17t AA/C Jones; 17c(i) Brand X Pics; 17c(ii) AA/M Chaplow; 17b AA/M Chaplow; 18t AA/M Chaplow; 18c(i) AA/J Edmanson; 18c(ii) AA/M Chaplow; 18b AA/J Edmanson; 19t AA/M Chaplow; 19c AA/M Chaplow; 19b AA/M Chaplow; 20/21 AA/J Edmanson; 24l AA/M Chaplow; 24/25t AA/M Chaplow; 24r AA/M Chaplow; 25bl AA/M Chaplow; 25br AA/M Chaplow; 26 Courtesy of Fundación MARQ; 27t Courtesy of Fundación MARQ; 27b Courtesy of Fundación MARQ; 28l AA/M Chaplow; 28t AA/M Chaplow; 28/29b AA/M Chaplow; 29t AA/M Chaplow; 29bl AA/M Chaplow; 29br AA/M Chaplow; 30l AA/J Edmanson; 30c AA/J Edmanson; 30r AA/M Chaplow; 31l AA/M Chaplow; 31r AA/M Chaplow; 32 Fotolincs/Alamy; 33t Fotolincs/Alamy; 33b Nature Picture Library/Alamy; 34 AA/M Chaplow; 34/35 AA/M Chaplow; 35r AA/M Chaplow; 36l AA/M Chaplow; 36c AA/M Chaplow; 36r AA/M Chaplow; 37 Caja Mediterráneo-Obras Sociales; 37 Caja Mediterráneo-Obras Sociales; 37 Caja Mediterráneo-Obras Sociales; 38–40 top panel AA/M Chaplow; 38l AA/M Chaplow; 39l AA/M Chaplow; 39r AA/M Chaplow; 40l AA/M Chaplow; 40r AA/M Chaplow; 41 AA/M Chaplow; 42 AA/M Chaplow; 43 AA/M Chaplow; 44–45 AA/C Sawyer; 46 AA/M Chaplow; 47–48 AA/C Sawyer; 49 AA/M Chaplow; 52l AA/M Chaplow; 52c AA/M Chaplow; 52r AA/M Chaplow; 53l AA/M Chaplow; 53r AA/M Chaplow; 54l AA/J Edmanson; 54tr AA/M Chaplow; 54br AA/J Edmanson; 55 AA/J Edmanson; 56l AA/J Edmanson; 56r AA/M Chaplow; 57 AA/J Edmanson; 58tl AA/M Chaplow; 58bl AA/J Edmanson; 58/59 AA/J Edmanson; 59 AA/M Chaplow; 60/61 AA/M Chaplow; 61t AA/M Chaplow; 61b AA/M Chaplow; 62 Javier Vázquez; 62/63 Javier Vázquez; 64 Javier Vázquez; 64l AA/S Watkins; 64/65t AA/M Chaplow; 64/65b AA/M Chaplow; 65 AA/M Chaplow; 66 AA/M Chaplow; 66/67 AA/M Chaplow; 67 AA/M Chaplow; 68 AA/M Chaplow; 69 AA/M Chaplow; 70–74 top panel AA/M Chaplow; 70l AA/M Chaplow; 70r AA/M Chaplow; 71l AA/M Chaplow; 71r AA/M Chaplow; 72 AA/M Chaplow; 73l AA/J Edmanson; 73r AA/M Chaplow; 74l AA/M Chaplow; 74r AA/M Chaplow; 75 AA/M Chaplow; 76 AA/M Chaplow; 77 AA/J Edmanson; 78 AA/M Chaplow; 79–80 AA/C Sawyer; 81–82 AA/C Sawyer; 83 AA/M Chaplow; 86 AA/M Chaplow; 87 AA/M Chaplow; 88l Javier Vázquez; 88r Javier Vázquez; 89l AA/M Chaplow; 89r AA/M Chaplow; 90/91t AA/M Chaplow; 90bl AA/M Chaplow; 90c AA/M Chaplow; 90/91b AA/M Chaplow; 91 AA/M Chaplow; 92t AA/J Edmanson; 92b AA/M Chaplow; 92–93 AA/M Chaplow; 93t AA/M Chaplow; 93 AA/M Chaplow; 94l AA/M Chaplow; 94r AA/M Chaplow; 95 AA/M Chaplow; 96–98 top panel AA/M Chaplow; 96l AA/J Edmanson; 96r AA/M Chaplow; 97l AA/M Chaplow; 97r AA/J Edmanson; 98l AA/M Chaplow; 98r AA/M Chaplow; 99 AA/M Chaplow; 100 AA/M Chaplow; 101 AA/M Chaplow; 102 AA/M Chaplow; 103 AA/C Sawyer; 104–106 AA/C Sawyer; 105 AA/J Edmanson; 107 AA/M Chaplow; 108–112 AA/C Sawyer; 108t AA/M Chaplow; 108c(i) AA/M Chaplow; 108c(ii) AA/M Chaplow; 108b AA/M Chaplow; 113 AA/J Edmanson; 114–125 top panel AA/M Chaplow; 118 AA/M Chaplow; 123 AA/M Chaplow; 124l AA; 124c AA/M Chaplow; 124r AA/M Chaplow; 125l AA/J Edmanson; 125c(i) AA/M Chaplow; 125c(ii) AA; 125r AA/M Chaplow.

Every effort has been made to trace the copyright holders, and we apologise in advance for any accidental errors. We would be happy to apply any corrections in the following edition of this publication.